WOMEN IN PANCHAYATI RAJ STRUCTURES

WOMEN IN PANCHAYATI RAJ STRUCTURES

By

P. Manikyamba

Foreword By

Dr. Vina Mazumdar

GYAN

Women in Panchayati Raj
Structures

ISBN: 978-81-212-0286-2

First Published 1989, reprint 2013 in India by
Gyan Publishing House
23, Main Ansari Road, Daryaganj,
New Delhi - 110002
Phones : 23282060, 23261060
Fax : (011) 23285914
E-mail: books@gyanbooks.com
website: gyanbooks.com

Printed at : Sagar Color Scan, New Delhi.

Foreword

THIS book is a commendable painstaking effort to assess women's participation in Panchayati Raj structures in India. There is a great dearth of material on this theme. A study of this type reflects the general nature of women's political participation in the country as a whole. The author's own micro-level studies of women's role in Panchayati Raj institutions in Andhra Pradesh have been the basis of her interest in pursuing data in other states on women's participation in grassroots political institutions. The author has analysed available but highly limited evidence for as many states as possible, and has had her tentative (?) generalisations supported by the studies of other scholars in the field. Her description of the problem could well be described as the tip of the iceberg.

The main conclusions of this study are supported by what we already know of the participation of women in various spheres. Women's political participation is much less than their work participation. The mass of rural women who form the majority of women in our country spend most of their time engaged in the battle for *survival*. They have little or no time at all for political activities. Furthermore, their low status in society, their low levels of literacy and awareness of their legal rights and responsibilities, and their ignorance of their purposes and procedures of Panchayati Raj institutions account for their low participation.

There is no lack of dynamism or leadership qualities among rural women, nor is it true that they are unaware of their own needs and those of development. Internalization of their subordinate status and culturally imposed constraints have made women diffident and fearful of taking part in the public affairs. In addition, they have been systematically passed over, not only by men in their families and villages but also by the agencies of the state and local power structures. They have been discouraged by traditional taboos, bullied, and used as proxies of men. The study contends that wherever exceptional women have been sighted, it is because they have had familial support, greater knowledge of the political process, education and higher levels of awareness and finally commitment. Women have proved to be active as well as effective in exercising power.

Panchayati Raj institutions have been virtually reduced to nullity except in a few states. The debate sparked off by the Constitution (sixty-fourth) Amendment Bill, 1989, has not so far touched the issue of expanding women's role in Panchayat bodies though the Bill includes a provision for increased reservation of seats for women. The book has thus come at a right time to generate some discussion on this issue.

As early as 1974, the Committee on the Status of Women in India had criticised the 'tokenism' displayed by provision of one seat for women in Panchayats all over the country. In the context of gross neglect of rural women's economic, social and political problems by all government institutions, the Committee had recommended the need for statutory Women's Panchayats with an integral connection with other Panchayat bodies. Unfortunately, this recommendation was never considered by the Government.

What has surfaced during the last 15 years through grassroots movements of women like Chipko, and intensive research on rural women's problems, capacities and attitudes is that peasant women have substantially different views and approaches to some of the burning problems like ecological imbalance and environmental degradation which are to a great extent the result of misguided development policies. Increasing realisation of this has forced even some of the major exponents of the 'Green Revolution' to exhort agricultural scientists and policy-makers to 'listen and learn' from poor rural women, as to what should be the future shape of agricultural and other aspects of rural development.

Had the voice of these peasant women been effective in developmental decisions earlier, perhaps many of the blunders of the past could have been avoided. The National Forest Policy 1988 also speaks about the need for a people's movement especially involving rural women in the restoration of forest cover.

The National Perspective Plan (NPP) for Women recommended the 30% reservation in Panchayat bodies mainly to expand rural women's opportunities for political participation. The national women's organisations which criticised many other elements in the NPP supported the need for reservation in Panchayat bodies, but insisted that they must be filled by election, with due care to ensure the representation of poor groups, especially Dalit and Adivasi women.

In today's context it is difficult to forecast the possible social and political implication or the outcome of the proposed Amendment.

Irrespective of the other implications of the Bill, however, the need to enhance peasant women's role in decisions that affect the state of natural and human resources in rural areas remain undisputed. Another issue that needs to be kept in mind is that resistance to women's participation and poor women in particular is highest at the lowest levels of rural power structures. Unless the compositions of the the Panchayats are radically transformed and the poor constitute a majority, it is doubtful whether the proposed enhancement of the powers of these bodies will really benefit women and other deprived groups in rural society.

How to prevent such a tragedy? What operative measures will prevent the measure advocated in the name of 'power to the people' from choking off people's power? Which people are we talking about? Even among women which category?

All these questions require not only reflection but close investigation of the behaviour of panchayat institution vis-a-vis women and other deprived groups. Unfortunately the massive research literature on Panchayati Raj built up by social scientists has rarely examined the women's dimension. From this point of view this book is a path breaker. I hope that other will follow this example.

Vina Mazumdar

Centre for Women's Development Studies
New Delhi
18th August 1989

Preface

THIS modest volume on Women in Panchayati Raj Structures is the sequel to the decision to amend the Indian Constitution providing for, among other things, thirty per cent seats in Panchayats for women with the possibility of this going upto fifty per cent as the Prime Minister stated. The Prime Minister also said that until women stood up and fight for their rights, the support from the government would not be useful. The coming elections to Lok Sabha and to the State Legislative Assemblies on the one hand and the raging distrust that has set in from the relations between the government and the opposition at the centre on the other arose, in some quarters, from misgivings about the motives of the government in giving effect to this important constitutional change. Doubts also would arise about women representatives of Panchayati Raj bodies playing useful roles even if membership is ensured by means of reservation. It is true that adequate women's representation in Panchayati Raj institutions is essential not only for ensuring political participation in the democratic process but also for realising the objectives of Panchayati Raj in general.

Indeed the attempt to strengthen democracy at the grassroots level through enhancing the representation of women, the most crucial segment of Indian society, is commendable. But the success of Panchayati Raj depends on adequate as well as effective participation of women in the rural processes. It is the decision of the government to expand and to ensure the role of rural women in Panchayati Raj and the interest of the author in the transformation of women's role in the social process in general that led to the writing of this book. The author has been engaged, for the past ten years, in investigating the role of women in Panchayati Raj institutions and the very recent changes in public policy in this area further inspired the writer's interest.

It is well recognised in public policy studies that programme appraisal should include both an assessment of past performance and an appraisal of the content and performance of new policies. Panchayati Raj in Indian States has been in existence for three decades following the recommendations of the Balwantrai Mehta

Committee which submitted its report in 1957. The important innovation of Panchayati Raj has been expected to 'usher in a truly democratic set up' and the integration of women in the process of development is regarded as important for the realisation of this objective. Hence a study of the role of women in Panchayati Raj set up is useful to assess the nature and pace of development in rural areas.

At the macro level, the book is concerned with an examination of the working of Panchayati Raj in general. An attempt is made by the author to identify the revitalisation trends present in the system. Special care is taken to study the role of women as beneficiaries and benefactors in the socio-economic and political processes of development.

At the micro level, the study concentrates on examining the recruitment pattern, awareness levels and the participatory position of the women members of the Panchayati Raj institutions in India. An attempt is also made to examine the relationship between the socio-economic background of women members and the participatory skills.

The contributing factors for active involvement and participation of women in the process of rural development have been identified. The study is also concerned with assessing the role of women presiding officers of the Panchayati Raj bodies. The structural, functional, attitudinal and environmental constraints for active involvement of rural women in the general social process and more importantly in the political process are discussed. The nature and extent of interaction of women of rural India, with the officials, the question of reservation of seats for women in the Panchayati Raj institutions, the type of functioning of women's organisations and the style of rural women's leadership are also discussed.

Do Indian women figure adequately in the rural development processes? Have the rural development programmes meant for women reached adequately? Could rural women come out of the cultural and environmental constraints to take effective roles in rural development? Are the profiles of rural women in the political field still marginal? Could the proposed Panchayati Raj Constitutional Amendment be regarded as a 'Perestroika' in the context of enhancing the political status of rural women? The author hopes that the study provides answers to at least some aspects of these questions.

P. Manikyamba

Acknowledgements

I am thankful to Professor R. V. R. Chandrasekhara Rao, Professor of Political Science, University of Hyderabad, for his valuable suggestions in conducting the study. I also benefited a lot through conducting discussions with my other colleagues in the department of Political Science on some of the issues dealt with in the book.

I am highly thankful to Dr Vina Majumdar, Director, Centre For Women's Development Studies, New Delhi for readily accepting to write the foreword.

I would like to thank the members of my family who helped me in many ways during my field work. They had to put up with my long periods of absence from home while my presence there was in fact needed.

My thanks are due to the officials of Panchayati Raj institutions which I had visited during my field work. I am especially indebted to the women members and women presiding officers of the Panchayati Raj bodies under study without whose cooperation the work would not have been completed.

To the staff of the National Institute of Rural Development, Hyderabad; Andhra Pradesh State Chamber of Panchayati Raj, Hyderabad; Bureau of Economics and Statistics, Hyderabad; Law Department Library, Andhra Pradesh Secretariat; University of Hyderabad Library, Hyderabad and the Osmania University Library, Hyderabad, I owe my thanks.

I am very much thankful to Sri R. Nagarajan, Stenotypist, Academic Staff College, University of Hyderabad for his patient, neat and quick typing.

I am particularly thankful to M/s Gian Publishing House, New Delhi, for readily accepting to bring out the book and for the quick processing of its publication.

Contents

1

Three Decades of Panchayati Raj

PANCHAYATI RAJ, one of the most important political innovations of independent India, is a channel for popular participation in the process of development. It is intended to function as a politico-administrative arrangement mostly to replace and, to an extent to adapt the patterns of colonial administration to the new polity. The team, appointed by the Government of India in January 1957 for the study of Community Projects and National Extension Service, popularly known as Balwantrai Mehta Committee, made far reaching recommendations in the direction of democratic decentralisation and rural reconstruction.[1] This Committee pointed out, in its report, that the least successful aspect of the Community Development Movement in India was its attempt to evoke local initiative and in the absence of local initiative and local interest, development would not be possible. The recommendations of the Committee were mainly concerned with the setting up of elected self-governing institutions; encouraging people's participation in community work; tribal development; cooperation; communication; promoting rural industries, health, education, agriculture and animal husbandry and promoting the welfare of weaker sections. The Committee had also made some recommendations in the direction of promoting the welfare of women.

The system of Panchayati Raj is expected to usher in a truly democratic set-up when once it is established on the lines expected by its promoters.[2] One writer has regarded Panchayati Raj as the heart of Indian politics[3] and it is hoped that the system would work as infinitely large number of lamps shedding their light around as a means of achieving comprehensive rural development and people's welfare.

The working of Panchayati Raj since 1959 has revealed several shortcomings as well as achievements. The fact is that the system has not broken down and certain trends of revitalisation are evident.[4] The system, in the opinion of one writer, has not forfeited the faith of the people, but has reached a stage of resurrection.[5] The following are some important benefits that the system brought about.

ACHIEVEMENTS

Social Change

It is true that Panchayati Raj has brought about some degree of social change. This is achieved both directly and indirectly. A study on Panchayati Raj and social change sponsored by the Government of Assam pointed out that while there are many variations in the performance of Panchayati Raj from place to place, its main role in changing the socio-economic life of the people cannot be denied. There has been a change in the value orientations of the people and in the leadership roles and Assam is moving towards modernisation under the impact of Panchayati Raj. Another study also in Assam made clear that elected leaders have shown high degree of participation and that there is enough evidence of the system's ability to establish its roots in the larger socio-political and administrative structure of the state. Elements of continuity which are vital for the growth of any organisation were noticed. The process of decision-making got accelerated and the value of Panchayati Raj in serving as link between rural masses and the government at higher levels got recognised.[6]

Increase in Consciousness and Awareness

One of the important achievements of Panchayati Raj is that it increased the consciousness of the people about their rights. Rural public, as it is noted in many studies, have become increasingly conscious of their social, economic and political rights. It is this consciousness and a feeling of asserting the rights that occasionally result in social tensions which, definitely, are marks of development. The findings of some of the studies would be worthwhile to mention here. One study on Political Transition in Rural Areas in Arunachal Pradesh made clear that with the introduction of Panchayati Raj in the state, individual voters became very conscious of their political role and also that a stir of women's political consciousness is occasionally felt in certain villages, especially at the time of Panchayati elections.[7]

The West Bengal Panchayat experiment evoked a nationwide interest and experiment. A study conducted on the working of some panchayats in West Bengal, bringing out the facts of the socio-political structures of the state, found out a high degree of political perception among the rural voter with no influence of caste in the socio-economic matrix. The new system has connected the rural people with the mainstream of national life in West Bengal.[8] In a study in the 1970s in three administrative divisions of West Bengal, as many as 1,214 respondents who form a large majority of the total number of respondents, admitted that the Panchayati Raj structures in West Bengal have been helpful in increasing the political awareness among the masses, making democracy more real to the common people, improving the lot of the poorer sections, making bureaucracy more responsive and creating a responsible and responsive leadership. Interestingly, it is only a very insignificant percentage of the respondents, only 1%, that favoured the idea of scrapping of Panchayati Raj institutions.[9] A favourable inclination among the public towards Panchayati Raj institutions was also found in a study sponsored by the National Institute of Public Cooperation and Child Development. This study pointed out that 70% of the respondents have high view of the Panchayati Raj institutions and implementation of their programmes. A high level of people's involvement in the working of the system is also made clear by the study.[10]

An increasing interest in activities like agricultural production, education, cooperation, social welfare and irrigation is found in the people of Gujarat.[11] In Haryana, Panchayati Raj made the rural masses more articulate. They have become more and more conscious of their rights, particularly about the right to vote, and also learnt the values of democracy. Evidence of politicization of rural society and re-structuring of groups cutting across religion, caste and other parochial barriers could be seen in this state.[12] In Tamil Nadu, in some villages, it was found that most of the villagers are aware of the existence of panchayats, and have a favourable orientation towards them and also towards the elected representatives. People in some villages regard the Panchayati Raj institutions as beneficial to the rural people.[13]

New Leadership

A significant contribution that the Panchayati Raj had made is that it has generated new leadership whether modern or semi-modern. A study on the emerging leadership in the Panchayati Raj system in Rajasthan said that a neo-traditional leadership has emerged in the State.[14] Another study pointed out that through Panchayati Raj, a truly local young leadership drawn from a wide range of occupational base has risen and that people belonging to backward classes had secured adequate representation in Panchayati Raj bodies.[15] West Bengal saw the emergence of a new youthful literate leadership,[16] and in this

State, the Panchayat leadership has been successful in mediating the interaction between tradition and modernity and playing an educative role *vis-a-vis* rural development.[17]

A study, conducted in the 60s in Maharashtra, showed that the social attitudes of a good number of leaders were congenial to communal harmony and social change. The leadership did show democratic and consultative character and there was no adversary relationship between the leaders and the followers.[18] It is also worth noticing that progressive sections came into leadership roles. The leadership pattern registered a shift, though of a limited nature. The authority of the old people, and the domination of upper social strata was found to have less of leverage in some places of Karnataka.[19] The young leadership is getting encouragement in some districts of Maharashtra. The leadership has also shown inclination in delegating authority which is crucial in the context of democratic functioning of the system. In addition, there has been a significant change in relation to the bases of legitimacy of leadership. The leadership in some places is very much respected and actions of the leaders are given recognition. A study of the working of Panchayati Raj pointed that a new secular perspective on the role of leaders and on their influence has emerged in the wake of Panchayati Raj.[20]

There have been instances when progressive leaders in village committees could overcome opposition from conservative force in villages. For example, in some villages of Rajasthan, the progressive chairman of village panchayats finally succeeded in overcoming the opposition emanating from groups consisting of money-lenders and grain-dealers in the matter of establishing a common centre for buying and selling seed grains and prevailed in doing so. The conclusion reached by the investigator of the study is that a strong leader could successfully fight the traditional pressure of village politics by maintaining a consistent position for a fairly long time.[21]

Uniform Pattern

The Panchayati Raj set-up has provided for a uniform pattern and infrastructure to implement rural development programmes. Their very existence filled a big organisational gap.

Emphasis on Developmental Role of Administrators

The Panchayati Raj system has also emphasised on the developmental role of administrators and the need for integrated rural development. Officials are expected to play the role of agents of change. With the introduction of Panchayati Raj, a number of officials like Block Development Officer, Mukhya Sevika, Grama Sevika, Social

Extension Officers in charge of health, education, social welfare and women welfare came into existence. These officials are also supposed to play the role of agents of awareness. It is important to point out that the enthusiastic reception and implementation of Panchayati Raj in the initial years was due to the highly supportive role of a number of officials, especially top civil servants, in different parts of the country.[22]

Democratic functioning

Some of the Panchayati Raj institutions in some states have earned reputation as efficient democratic structures. For instance, in Maharashtra, the Zilla Parishads, one study pointed out, have created a place for themselves as democratic institutions in the body politic.[23] It has also been pointed out that frequent meetings of Village Panchayats and Panchayat Samithis have brought together members of different part of the rural areas who have really put forth their energies and enthusiasm to tackle long standing problems of development. The same study further noted that the participation of the people's representatives in the rural institutions, especially in the discussion of policy matters and decision making is decidedly conducive to the promotion of democracy. The committee system has been found very effective. In spite of occasional stress and strain, balance could be struck in the relationship between elected office bearers and civil servants.[24]

Diffused Elite

While it is true that the Panchayati Raj bodies in general are dominated by socially and economically dominant classes, evidence to the contrary is also available. In West Bengal, the village elite formerly confined to upper classes is now more widely diffused. In Andhra Pradesh too, there has been a distinct shift away from the traditional land-owning type of leadership towards one which is economically of a lower middle class background.[25] In Rajasthan, a truly local leadership of the age group of below 40 and drawn from a wide occupational base is reported to have emerged.[26]

Factionalism, Not a Continuous Hurdle

Factionalism, viewed from a negative perspective is harmful for the effective functioning of any system. But provided there is an attempt to reduce its impact or even to eliminate it, would not be a big hindrance for the smooth running of a system. This attempt has been really made in some places of Andhra Pradesh. In the Pendurti Panchayati Samithi in 60s, factional politics based on caste and regional considerations have been obvious before and during elections, but astonishingly enough, have been forgotten after elections. The way in which the meetings of the Samithi and its Standing Committees were conducted by the Samithi presidents and also the manner of participation of various members showed without doubt that the Samithi worked well as a democratic institution despite the fact that there were factions at the time of Samithi elections. The spirit of public services and the democratic approach of the president of the Samithi was found responsible, mainly for this pleasant state of affairs.[27]

From the above, it is clear that the Panchayati Raj set-up in India has not proved to be a total failure. In essence, as the Ashok Mehta Committee, appointed by the Government of India in 1977 to study the working of this system, concluded "politically speaking it became a process of democratic seed-drillng in the Indian soil by making an average citizen conscious of his rights than before. Administratively speaking, it bridged the gulf between the bureaucratic elite and the people. Sociologically speaking, it generated a new leadership which is not merely relatively young in age but also modernistic and pro-social change in outlook. Finally, looked at from the developmental angle, it helped rural people to cultivate a developmental psyche".[28]

SHORTCOMINGS

The lamps that shed lights around the Panchayati Raj set up have not been infinite and the system has only proved to be a partial success. This situation is due to some important factors mentioned below.

Domination by Socially and Economically Privileged Classes

The domination of the Panchayati Raj institutions by the economically and socially privileged classes has often been mentioned as important cause for not realising the goals of Panchayati Raj. This could be illustrated. A study conducted in Karnataka made clear that the weaker groups still live in the same economic dependence, deep ignorance of their rights and despite statutory membership in Panchayati Raj institutions, these groups show themselves as 'show pieces' and that the Government is satisfied with the existing situation.[29] Another assessment was that the power structure in the system is heavily in favour of the locally dominant social groups, dominated especially by upper economic classes.[30]

Philosophy not Properly Understood

A clear understanding among the functionaries of the philosophy behind any innovation is very important to its successful working. But precisely in this context, leaving some exceptions, we notice a big lapse. In some parts of Bihar, it is found that neither the rural civil servants nor the Panchayati Raj non-officials seem to have been aware, much less imbibed, the philosophy of the system. The objectives of Panchayati Raj are being comprehended and interpreted differently by these two partners in the system. The introduction of democratic decentralisation has become something like an imposition of democratic structures upon a traditional social structure. The generality of local leadership had shown little commitment to development and to the democratic process.[31]

Absence of awareness of the system in general and the institutions as well their functions in particular would result in slow progress or no progress. In a large number of Panchayati Raj institutions, awareness of majority of members is found lacking. To cite one example, the political leadership and membership in a Samithi in Andhra Pradesh were not aware of the importance of the social, economic and political goals of Panchayati Raj institutions and these representatives did not also have any developmental orientation.[32] A study in Assam reported that the respondents do not have a clear idea about the nature and organisation of Panchayati Raj and the objectives and roles which it is expected to play in promoting rural development.[33]

Qualitatively Weak Membership

Apart from the size of any organization or institution, its successful functioning depends upon the quality of membership. Unfortunately, in this matter of recruiting able and committed members, the Indian electorate has not taken reasonable care. The attitude of the people, viewed at a macro level analysis, is one of indifference, and nil participation. This is found to be true in many parts of India. A study conducted on Community Development in Kerala made this point vividly clear.[34]

Unenthusiastic Attitude of Ex-officio Members

In a majority of Indian States, in the district and middle level institutions, ex-officio membership is provided for by the relevant Acts. This results in the inclusion of MPs, MLAs and MLCs as ex-officio members in these bodies. In fact, these members could be effective channels of communication between the State and local level political institutions. In the initial years of the functioning of Panchayati Raj bodies, the participation of these members was significant. But their enthusiasm relatively cooled down, as the Ashok Mehta Committee reported, and their participation is often marked by absence than presence in these bodies. The reason for the lowering in interest and enthusiasm in the ex-officio members could be the fear that encouraging the principles of devolution, decentralisation, local initiative and decision would weaken their own position as popular representatives of these areas, and these state and central level legislators also got scared that people would look forward to local leadership itself for the redressal of their grievances and for the development of the villages in general. Similar views were expressed by the Singhvi committee in its report on Panchayati Raj institutions. The committee pointed out that the potential of Panchayati Raj institutions as people's centres aroused apprehensions and this resulted in the creation of a jealous hostility around. The committee further said that the elected representatives in Parliament and state assemblies using labours, in spite of the fact that their dependence on Panchayati Raj functionaries was inevitable, were not willing to share power with them.[35]

Unsatisfactory Bureaucratic Response

One of the main reasons for the unimpressive performance of Panchayati Raj is the attitude of bureaucracy. The bureaucracy in general, has failed to shed its elitist approach, feeling of superiority and general contempt for the illiterate and semi-literate villagers. This does not mean that the political executive has always tried to win the sympathy, understanding and respect of the officials. This is only to suggest that bureaucracy played its own part in retarding the role of Panchayati Raj Institutions in the process of development. There is ample evidence to support this. One study pointed out how conflict-situations between local political bodies and the officials arise due to socio-psychological factors, and how rude and unhelpful could the bureaucrats be in their behavioural patterns.[36] The bureaucrats, have found difficult, on one hand, as the Ashok Mehta Committee pointed out, to assume additional responsibilities and later became averse to them, and on the other could not get easily adjusted to work under the elected representatives. A tendency of upward deference, a tendency to conform their behaviour to the expectations of their superiors, but not to those of the popular representatives, could be seen in the officials.[37] There is evidence of the administrators' low esteem of politics and political leaders, a tendency to recognise themselves and not the political leaders as decision-makers and of a refusal to recognise the importance of special interests in democratic politics. The bureaucrats very often see themselves as instruments of implementation and see democracy as hampering their work and have a general suspicion of the environment and hostility towards politicians. This attitude strongly comes in the way of their commitment to the whole Panchayati Raj ideology.[38]

Thus unwillingness of bureaucracy to become rural-oriented,[39] the self-justification, self-perpetuation, and self-assertion visible in the behavioural pattern[40] contributed considerably to the decline of Panchayati Raj. In addition, local vested interests and the elected legislators, both MLAs and MPs also contributed to cripple and eventually discard Panchayati Raj. Consequently the bureaucracy gained upper hand in a grand alliance with the state and central level political elite[41] gradually making the system of Panchayati Raj ineffective.

Factionalism

The phenomenon of factionalism, except in some places and institutions has become an inhibiting factor for the proper functioning of Panchayati Raj. There have been several occasions when factionalism led to the suspension of popularly elected bodies, a total halt in developmental works and strained social relations. According to one report, factionalism became extensively pervasive in the Jaipur district of Rajasthan.[42] The rivalries arising out of factionalism told on harmony among villagers.

Structural and Functional Factors

The effective functioning of Panchayati Raj system is conditioned by some structural and functional constraints. Unclear demarcation of the spheres of action of the appointed and elected members, concentration of authority in and the exercise of power by the presiding officers, prevalence of mistrust and suspicion in the political and executive wings, dual control on the officials could be included in this category of constraints. These constraints will come in the way of the grass-roots democratic institutions' growth.

State Governments' Attitude

As the Ashok Mehta Committee pointed out, the niggardly attitude of the State Governments towards Panchayati Raj institutions is responsible for their very limited success. The attitude is marked by 'paternalism' according to one study in Andhra Pradesh. The autonomy of these institutions which is an important ingredient for democratic decentralisation is conditioned by the ambivalent attitude of state governments. On one hand, there appears a realisation that in view of large scale development programmes, decentralisation of powers to local leaders is necessary and on the other there seems to be suspicion and fear that such power would reduce the status of state governments and that the local authorities would misuse the power entrusted to them.[43]

Inadequate Funds

The paucity of funds is yet another and important factor in the failure of successful running of Panchayati Raj machinery. The writer has observed, on various occasions, that the limited resources available to the Panchayati Raj institutions create tension situations. For instance, a President of a Mandala Praja Parishad in Andhra Pradesh found it very difficult to find a solution in a situation of a limited amount available for loans sanction and hundreds of applicants.

The Present Phase of Panchayati Raj

The above discussion would give rise to two questions — Is it necessary to scrap the Panchayati Raj system? Is revitalisation not desirable? In this connection the assessments of some experts in Panchayati Raj deserve consideration. According to the incisive assessment of Panchayati Raj system by the Ashok Mehta Committee, the system passed through three phases — the phase of Ascendence (1959-64), the phase of Stagnation (1965-69) and the phase of Decline (1970-75).[44] According to an assessment made in 1986, the first phase between 1959-67 could be regarded as bright, the second phase from 1967-76 turned to be bleak and in the third starting from 1977 steps have been introduced to revitalise Panchayati Raj.[45] A study of the role of women in Panchayati Raj by the writer also points out that the post-1977 phase of Panchayati Raj could hopefully be viewed as the revitalisation phase. The fact is that, there is ample evidence to suggest that the system has not broken down and trends of revitalisation are evident.

As Lakshmi Chand Jain, who served on several expert committees constituted by the Government of India said in an interview, "the fault does not lie in those bodies but it is a reflection of our failure to match their responsibilites with adequate resources of man power including technical man power and funds."[46] An important Committee, popularly known as G.V.K. Rao Committee, which reviewed the administrative arrangements for Rural Development and Poverty Alleviation Programmes reported that "in order that the felt needs of the local people and the area are articulated for planning, priorities are established and effectively implemented, there is no better instrument to meet the needs other than the Panchayati Raj institutions. These institutions need to be revitalised and endowed with necessary resources and powers to discharge the functions and responsibilities assigned to them.[47] Efforts in the direction of revitalisation at the structural-functional levels of Panchayati Raj bodies and also at the level of performance of Panchayati Raj programmes would definitely bring about desired benefits. What is very importantly required is real commitment and motivation, the promotion of which should not be an impossible task.

References

1. Government of India, Committee on Plan Projects, Report of the Team for the Study of Community Projects and National Extension Service, 1957, Vol. I, p.1.
2. Reddy, Ram, Social Composition of Panchayati Raj: Background of Political Executives in Andhra, *Economic and Political Weekly*, Vol. II, 1967, p. 2214.
3. Arjun Y Darshankar, *Leadership in Panchayati Raj: A study of Beed District*, Panchasheel Prakashan, Jaipur, 1979, p. 1.
4. Manikyamba, P., Women in Panchayati Raj: Premises and Performance, A paper presented at a Seminar on District Administration organised in March 1988 by Shaheed Bhagat Singh College, New Delhi, (unpublished).
5. Lakshminarayana H.D., *Rural Legislators in an Indian State*, Inter-India Publications, New Delhi, 1985, p. 310.
6. (a) Jain S.P., and Naidu, N.Y., Panchayati Raj and Social Change: A study in Assam, National Institute of Rural Development, (unpublished), 1978, pp. 97-99. (b) Jain, S.P., Panchayati Raj in Assam, National Institute of Community Development, Hyderabad, 1976, p. 114
7. Talunkar Atul Chandra, *Political Transition in Grassroots in Tribal India*, Omsons Publications, New Delhi, 1987, p. 200.
8. Government of West Bengal, Dept. of Panchayats and Community Development, Panchayats in West Bengal from 1978-79 to 1980-81, A Review, Jan, 1982. pp. 10-14.
9. *Ibid.* p. 22.
10. Sugata Dasgupta & L.S.N. Murthy, *Panchayati Raj Institutions in West Bengal*, National Institute of Public Cooperation and Child Development, New Delhi, 1983, pp. 38-39.
11. Vakil F.D., Panchayati Raj in Gujarat, Ram Reddy G. (ed) *Patterns of Panchayati Raj in India*, The Macmillan Company of India Ltd., New Delhi, 1977, p. 106
12. Ranbir Singh, Panchayati Raj in Haryana, *Ibid*, p. 126-127.
13. Subramanian, Panchayati Raj in Tamilnadu, *Ibid.* p. 272.
14. Bhargava, B.S., *Emerging Leadership in Panchayati Raj System, A study in a District of Rajasthan*, Institute for Social and Economic Change, Bangalore, 1977, p. 41.
15. Iqbal Narain and P.C. Mathur's report on Panchayati Raj in the Jaipur district of Rajasthan cited by Mats, Khilberg in *The Panchayati Raj of*

India: Debate in a Developing Country, Young Asia Publications, New Delhi, 1976, p. 90.

16. Government of West Bengal, Panchayats in West Bengal from 1978-79 to 1980-81, a Review, *op. cit.* p. 14.
17. *Ibid.* p. 19.
18. Inamdar, N.R., Functioning of Village Panchayats in Maharashtra, Jacob George (ed), *Readings on Panchayati Raj,* National Institute of Community Development, Hyderabad, 1967, pp. 27-47.
19. Laxminarayana, H.D., *Rural Legislators in an Indian State,* Inter Asia Publications, New Delni, 1985, p. 71.
20. Jain, S.P., Panchayati Raj in Punjab, (ed) Ram Reddy, *Patterns of Panchayati Raj, op. cit.* p. 259.
21. Sharma, Prabhu Datta cited by Mats, Kihlberg in *The Panchayati Raj of India: Debate in a Developing Country, op. cit,* Young Asia Publications, New Delhi, 1970, pp. 68-69.
22. Shivayya M, *Panchayati Raj: A Policy Perspective,* National Institute of Rural Development, Hyderabad, 1986, p. 8.
23. Inamdar, N.R., Panchayati Raj in Maharashtra, (ed) G. Ram Reddy, *Patterns of Panchayati Raj, op. cit.* pp. 192-195.
24. Planning Commission, Programme Evaluation Organisation, *Some Successful Panchayats: Case Studies,* 1960.
25. Shivayya, M., *op. cit.* p. 13.
26. Narain, Iqbal and Mathur, P.C., *Readings on Panchayati Raj* (ed) Jacob George. National Institute of Community Development, Hyderabad, 1967, p. 90.
27. Sarveswara, Rao B. and Ramana, K.V., *Panchayat Samithis: A Case Study in Andhra Pradesh* (ed) Jacob George, *Ibid,* p. 68.
28. Government of India, Report of the Committee on Panchayati Raj, 1978, p. 8.
29. Parvatamma, C., Panchayati Raj and Weaker Sections, a paper presented at a Seminar organised in 1975 by the National Institute of Community Development, cited by Mats Kihlberg, *The Panchayati Raj of India, Debate in a Developing Country, op. cit.* p. 96.
30. Raghava Rao, *Panchayats and Rural Develpment,* Asish Publishing House, New Delhi, 1980, pp. 77-78.
31. Haridwar Rai, A., and Awadesh Prasad, Panchayati Raj in Bihar, (ed) Ram Reddy, *Patterns of Panchayati Raj, op. cit.* p. 89.

32. Haragopal, G., *Administrative Leadership and Rural Development in India*, Light and Life Publishers, New Delhi, 1980. p. 180.
33. Jain, S.P. *Panchayati Raj in Assam, op. cit.* pp. 117-118.
34. Panikkar, K.K., *Community Development in Kerala*, S. Chand & Co. Pvt. Ltd., New Delhi, 1974. p.212.
35. Extracts published in Kurukshetra, Vol. XXXVII, No. 5, Feb. 1989, p. 41.
36. Gaikwad, V.R., *Panchayati Raj and Bureaucracy: A Study of the Relationship Pattern*, National Institute of Community Development, Hyderabad, 1969, pp. 64-70.
37. Shanti Kothari and Ramashray Roy, *Relation between Politicians and Administrators at the District Level*, Indian Institute of Public Administration, New Delhi, 1981, pp. 163-165.
38. Mathu,r Kuldeep, *Bureaucratic Response to Development*, National Publishing House, New Delhi, 1972, pp. 58-59 and 89.
39. Working Paper on the Panchayati Raj Institutions issued by the Committee Appointed by the Govt. of Andhra Pradesh on Panchayati Raj Institutions, 1981, pp. 9.
40. Chandrasekhara Rao, R.V.R., Some Aspects of Reorganisation of District Administration in Andhra Pradesh, *Journal of the Society for the Study of State Governments*, Vol. II, Oct-Dec. 1969, p. 219.
41. Mathew George, *Panchayati Raj in Karnataka Today*, Institute of Social Sciences and Concept Publishing Company, New Delhi, 1986, pp. 8-9.
42. Narain, Iqbal and Mathur, P.C. Panchayati Raj in Rajasthan: A case study in Jaipur Dist., (ed.) Jacob George, *Readings on Panchayati Raj, op. cit.* p. 94.
43. Ram Reddy, G. (ed) Panchayati Raj in Andhra Pradesh in *Patterns of Panchayati Raj, op. cit.* p. 42.
44. Government of India, Report of the Committee on Panchayati Raj, *op. cit.* p. 4.
45. Shivayya, M., Panchayati Raj: A Policy Perspective, *op. cit.* pp. 8-11.
46. Interview by Nirmal Ganguli, Kurukshetra, Vol. XXXVII, No. 5, Feb. 1989, p. 51.
47. Government of India, Department of Rural Development, Ministry of Agriculture, Report of the Committee to Review the existing Administrative Arrangements for Rural Development and Poverty Alleviation Programmes, Dec. 1985, p. 41.

2

Panchayati Raj and Rural Women

THE makers of Panchayati Raj system desired that rural women should not only become beneficiaries of development, but more importantly contributors to it. The Balwantrai Mehta Committee considered the conditions of rural women at length and felt that they should be assisted to find ways to increase their incomes and improve the conditions of their children.[1] In fact, a section of the report deals with the measures to be taken in this regard. The efforts should be, according to the Committee, in the direction of designing smokeless *chullhas*, providing for personal and environmental cleanliness, taking care of the cattle, developing kitchen gardens, learning poultry keeping, training in the elementary use of thread and needle so that women could mend clothes for the family and organising cooking classes. In the opinion of the Committee, appointment of separate staff which should include Women Social Extension Officers and Gram Sevikas is very much needed for carrying out the phased welfare programmes meant for women.[2] But the activities suggested by the Committee in the section with the title "Work Among Women and Children" are not really income-generating and are only meant for house-keeping. The Committee was particular that women should find representation in the rural political institutions. Hence it recommended the cooperation of women members to the Panchayati Raj institutions.[3]

The next major landmark for Panchayati Raj is the Ashok Mehta Committee Report which was in the nature of a public policy appraisal of not only of rural governmental institution but also of comprehensive rural development itself. This Committee laid special emphasis on the need to reorganise and strengthen women's constructive decision making and managerial roles. The Committee categorically stated that the introduction of Panchayati Raj has added an important dimension to the role of rural women and that the importance of women's role in decision-making on development projects has been brought to the forefront. The Committee specifically recommended the promotion of women's role in rural industrialisation as a means of providing employment for women. The Committee suggested that arrangements should be made to ensure financial assistance to women and to facilitate and promote self-employment. The Committee also laid stress on the effective organisation of Mahila Mandals as important components in the rural development programmes. It also felt that rural women should have full access to development resources and services and pointed out that the motivational and promotional role of Panchayati Raj will be crucial in this area. The body also recommended that a Committee with all the women members of the Mandal Panchayats represented on it, should be formed so that decisions are made by women members themselves on priorities and choices in welfare and development programmes meant for women and children.[4] The Committee considered women as the 'most important part of our population' and felt that women should not become losers in the process of development.

Now the question is — have the rural women really become beneficiaries of and contributors to development? The answer can neither be a categorical 'Yes' nor a categorical 'No'. A study of the policies and programmes meant for rural women's development and their implementation would make the point clear.

National Policy on Rural Women's Development

Rural Women in India constitute nearly 80% of the female population. Their development as already pointed out, has been recognised as crucial in the overall development of the country in general and in that of the rural areas in particular. A systematic analysis and examination of the status and role of women in rural development strategies in India, as mentioned in the National Perspective Plan for Women, started with the National Plan of Action for Women (1976)[5]. The National Plan of Action laid emphasis on promoting village industries which provide scope for the employment of women, providing special training services and providing credit and marketing facilities to the goods produced by rural women. The National Plan of Action also contained legislative, administrative and other measures to be taken by the Government of India to improve the status of Indian women in general. The Plan also suggested the introduction of implementation machinery. It should be pointed out here that the preparation of the National Plan of Action was largely due to the influence of the report of the Committee on the Status of Women in India. The need for greater efforts for the emancipation of women was largely felt in the period following 1975 (the International Women's Year) and hence a chapter on Women and Development was included in the Sixth Five Year Plan (1980-85). Consequently, women activists, researchers and social scientists in India brought to focus the need for reorientation of programmes for women's development and also the need for rethinking on women's role in society as both beneficiaries and benefactors. The strategy to be adopted under the Sixth Plan was therefore — education, employment and health which are interdependent. The economic emancipation of the family with specific attention to women and education of children and family planning constituted the three major operational aspects of the family centred poverty alleviation strategy under the Sixth Plan. The Government decided to take steps to create a general awareness and understanding of the problems of women, strengthen voluntary action at the grassroots level, promote village level organisations like Mahila Mandals, expand functional literacy programmes, expand minimum health facilities, improve nutrition status, provide fair share of employment opportunities, identify the specific needs and problems of self-employed women, extend support to self-employed women and to expand and diversify education and training opportunities for women. As Part of the Sixth Plan rural development strategy, the National Scheme of Training Rural Youth for Self-Employment (TRYSEM), is also expected to cover a large number of rural women.[6]

In the Seventh Plan period the basic approach of the Government "would be to inculcate confidence among women and bring about an awareness of their own potential for development, as also of their rights and privileges".[7] The Plan envisages giving special attention to improve the existing skills of women and imparting to them new skills under the farmer's training, exchange of development, fodder production, post harvest technology, application of pesticides, budding and grafting, farmers' training in horticulture, fisheries, poultry, dairy, social forestry, etc. During the Seventh Plan, it is also decided that importance would be given to achieve a larger coverage of women in the Integrated Rural Development Programmes. It is also decided to strengthen all the existing programmes meant for women's development. It is important to note that a new scheme, namely the creation of Women's Development Corporations, is proposed to be taken up for promoting employment generating activities. These corporations would identify potential areas of employment and assist women in project formulation, raising finances and marketing of their products. The setting up of a Women's Development Planning and Monitoring Cell intended for collection of data and monitoring of plan programmes is also included. In addition, special cells in various

Ministries to ensure proper monitoring and coordination of different schemes are envisaged.[8]

Following the Sixth and Seventh Plans, the Department of Rural Development issued directions to State Governments to enhance the share of women under the Integrated Rural Development Programmes and to give priority to those households headed by women.

It is clear from the above that the government realised the fact that the benefits of the Rural Development Programmes would not reach women adequately unless specific earmarking of schemes and funds are made and special efforts are taken to integrate women in the mainstream of development. It is important to mention that the problems of women in the post-independence period came to be noticed reasonably since the 70s and serious thoughts to solve the problems and improve their status is being given in the 80s.

Programmes

Women of rural areas could get the benefit of all the programmes intended for rural developments in general. In addition to this, benefits could be derived from some special programmes evolved to meet the requirements of rural women. The following are some of the details.

Under the Integrated Rural Development Programme, (initiated in 1978-79) the chief objectives of which are income generation and providing credit facilities and subsidies. It is envisaged that at least 30% of the beneficiaries should be women. To realise this, stress is to be laid on giving adequate employment to women under the National Rural Employment Programme and Rural Landless Employment Guarantee Scheme. It is also decided that a minimum of one third of the beneficiaries under the scheme, Training of Youth for Self-Employment (TRYSEM), would be women.

An exclusive scheme called Development of Women and Children in Rural Areas (DWCRA) intended for the social and economic uplift of women belonging to families below the poverty line was launched in 1982 as a sub-component of Integrated Rural Development Programme. The salient features of this scheme are: group approach and organising the women of identified families into groups of 15 to 20 each for taking up income generating activities suited to their skills and aptitudes. These activities include weaving, fish vending, broom and rope making, brick making, pickle making, candle making and baking. In this scheme, traditional skills would be supplemented by training imparted under TRYSEM. The training is intended to be imparted in the Multi-Purpose Community Centres that would be set up in DWCRA blocks and funds for these centres would be made available from the Rural Employment Generation Programmes. Each Multi-purpose Community Centre is designed to provide for a training-cum-demonstration hall, *balwadi* for children and living accommodation for the Gram Sevika. Each Centre would be given assistance for equipment up to Rs. 50,000/- by the UNICEF. The government of India has also taken a policy decision of entrusting the overall responsibility of training the DWCRA functionaries to the National Institute of Rural Development, Hyderabad, Andhra Pradesh, from the financial year 1988-89. To supplement the efforts of government in benefiting rural women under the programme and to get wider coverage, it is decided to make funds available to voluntary agencies who take up projects in conformity with the DWCRA guidelines.

In addition to the above schemes, the Accelerated Rural Water Supply Programme and the Minimum Needs Programme are also intended to be of special significance to rural women who are the victims of drudgery.

Women are now treated as the targets of the awareness-creation programmes as well as the agents for creating awareness in conservation of water and maintenance of water sources. The Low Cost Sanitation Programme also gives importance to women. The programmes aimed at promoting rural technology are intended to relieve the drudgery of women in daily domestic and outside activities. Under a more directly targeted scheme — Science and Technology for Women, development of smokeless *chullahs,* use of solar cookers and setting up of bio-gas plants and devices for improving the water purification system are intended to be taken up.

Under social forestry programmes, it is decided to give "Tree Pattas" in the name of women.[9]

The scheme of Krishi Vigyan Kendras (introduced in the Sixth Plan period) for bridging the gap between the farmer's knowledge and available technology also covers women.

The programmes also include those concerning Functional Literacy for Adult Women and Health and Nutrition. In essence, the focus in the programmes has shifted from *welfare to development.*

The Reality

A look at the policies and programmes concerning rural women's development in India should not lead one to conclude that rural women could get real benefit out of these programmes and that rural women's status has improved considerably. The following discussion would make this point clear.

Rural Women and Education

Education is an important means of preparing individuals to effectively contribute to the socio-economic development of the country, to strengthen their role in society and to realise their own capacity. Unfortunately, education of women in general and rural women in particular has not progressed considerably in our country. Though the literacy rate for women has increased, it is not a satisfactory increase. Among women of rural India, only 12.92% and 17.96% were literates in 1971 and 1981 respectively as against 27.37% and 47.82% of urban women in the same years. The percentage of rural literate women in some States of India is more than that of the national percentage. For example in West Bengal 18.82% and 22.06% of rural women were literates according to the Census Reports of 1971 and 1981. In Karnataka, the percentage of rural literate women in 1971 and 1981 were 16.74 and 19.77. Only a negligible percentage of rural women receive education beyond primary level. According to one study, education to women is considered as an ornament while its utility is not recognised.[10]

Rural Women and Employment

Women's employment has been regarded as the 'critical entry point' for women's integration in mainstream development. Rural women in India spend longer hours in unpaid domestic work. A study on women of Rural Asia while pointing out the minimum and maximum contribution of men and women to domestic work underscores the fact that women devote 17 hours a day in work related to cooking, fuel collection, washing utensils, child care, sweeping and such other activities.[11] 83% of women participate in agriculture and other allied activities like dairying, animal husbandry, fisheries, sericulture, handlooms, handicrafts and forests. A sizeable portion of women are involved in construction activities. As pointed out in the Report of the National Commission on Self-employed Women and Women in the Informal Sector, "Women of the unorganised sector do not have the necessary visibility and do not get the focus of attention of the planners and implementers."[12]

The contribution of women in agricultural operations such as sowing, weeding, transplantation and harvesting is substantial. Yet this scarcely gets recognised by the immediate society, thus further leading to the loss of morale of rural women and to confirm and perpetuate the perceptions of low self-esteem and low achievement on their part. Women employed in agriculture suffer from wage discrimination. Their say in decision-making and marketing is near nil. With the process of deforestation, the task of collecting fuel and fodder by rural women has become more strenuous and the social forestry programme of the Government has not increased the employment opportunities for women.

Rural women have become only marginally visible in the antipoverty programmes. The share of employment generated under National Rural Employment Programme for Women is only approximately 20%.[13] Women's role has not been adequately recognised in rural industrialisation too. They still remain unequal partners in development.

The rate of skill formation among females of rural areas is estimated at only 3.3% according to 1981 census. The female work-force participation in rural areas is only 16.5% according to the same estimates. It is very important to note that though women constitute a major work force in agriculture, they are invisible in the Training Programmes. As pointed out in one study, the stress should be on improving the available skills and opportunities and also on developing new skills so that women could become effective organisers in the 'dynamic environment' of rural areas.[14]

As pointed out earlier, poverty alleviation in the rural sector is the central theme of the Seventh Plan. In the case of women, special care is intended to be taken to bring out women-headed households (estimated to be 30.35% in rural areas) above the poverty line. The instances of females heading households arise under special circumstances in a patriarchical society. Instances of females heading households could be due to migration of the male head of the family to another place, widowhood, separation or destitution or divorce. The presence of handicapped male heads of family and the male members' unwillingness to work and contribute to family also sometimes lead to the females taking the responsibility of heading the families. Available evidence suggests that the flow of assistance to women headed households has been very marginal.[15] The number of women headed families receiving benefit under IRDP during 1986-87 amounted to 15.23%, the target being 30%. It is also found that women heads of households face discrimination in getting institutional credit, and access to modern technology.[16] The achievements of the scheme DWCRA are encouraging. During 1982-87, 11,553 women groups are reported to have been organised in 106 districts under this scheme. The training of women under TRYSEM has exceeded the target to 44%, the target being 30%.

Rural Women and Technology

Rural women's access to technology is limited. In addition to the general bias against the use of technology by women, there is more bias against its use by rural women. Existing evidence shows that technology has not reached rural women adequately and women's access to management training and subsequent placement in good employment are less heard of.[17] The development of technology, surprisingly, has brought about adverse effects on rural women's lives and has displaced them from their work in several cases. For example, technology change in the case of fishing sector, one study pointed out, changed the labour processes and appropriated the tools of production into male hands.[18] Women who were engaged in hand-block printing in Jaipur and Ahmedabad are thrown out of employment on account of the introduction of screen printing method adopted by a few resourceful entrepreneurs. It is to be pointed out here that these now jobless women do not go out of their homes to learn screen printing because cultural constraints prevent them to do so. They now remain stay-at-home women.[19] Women agents of lace exporters in the West Godavari District of Andhra Pradesh who walk to distant villages to collect lace are increasingly replaced by men on bicycles who can collect lace in less time.

Women's Leadership

Effective leadership of women is important for bringing them into the mainstream of development. Leadership of women at the grassroots level, in general, is unsatisfactory. As pointed out by one writer, the qualities expected and appreciated in a woman have not included leadership, dynamism, initiative, independence, drive or organising ability.[20] Hence such qualities have been suppressed and woman has been so brought up as to consider them undesirable. But some recent trends in States like Andhra Pradesh reveal that a new young women's leadership is emerging. During her recent field work in Andhra Pradesh, the writer noticed that some women leaders are very active and committed. This situation is definitely an encouraging one. It makes one to think that training of women to become responsible leaders will add momentum to the already existing encouraging trend. It should be mentioned here that in some countries such training facilities are provided. For example, at Nsamizi in Uganda a multi-purpose training centre was established to train women leaders and to train men and women community development workers. In Guyana, women's institutions to educate women for assuming leadership roles got established. In Japan, groups called Living Improvement Groups mainly composed of women in rural communities, help to plan projects for their improvement. Thailand launched programme to train women leaders who would help rural women to organise themselves into groups.[21]

Viewed from a macro-level, women's leadership in the rural political scene also reveals an unhappy situation. But micro-level studies help us identify some shining stars. The writer found that some women presidents of Mandala Praja Parishads in Andhra Pradesh, (9% of the offices of President of Mandala Praja Parishads and Zilla Praja Parishads in Andhra Pradesh is reserved for women) are functioning as effective leaders. A number of women participated in the election campaign of these presidents. Thus reservation of key positions to women when purposefully utilised have yielded beneficent results. As pointed out in the National Perspective Plan for Women, power and access to positions of decision-making and authority are critical pre-requisites for women's equality in the process of nation building.[22] It should be noted that there have been occasions when women were prevented from participating even in the most elementary stage of participation, namely voting in elections. For instance in 1965, in Pipliyakhurd village in the Jhalawada district of Rajasthan the male villagers decided to disallow women to vote in the Gram Panchayat elections. Surprisingly, it was their strong belief that success in elections with the support of women voters was insignificant and that defeat without their support was better than success that apparantly led to such a decision.[23] A comparison of a situation of this type with the one where women have assumed active roles in key position enables one to identify and acknowledge the progress of women in local politics, though the fact remains that political women in key roles are only a few in number.

Women's Organisations

Viable women's organisations would help women to develop confidence and to engage in collective action. As one study pointed out, fundamental change requires organisation. Organisation in turn enables women to achieve full and equal partnership in development and to work for the construction of a more equitable, healthy and prosperous society.[24] Unfortunately, in the context of organising themselves, women in general are lagging behind. A study on the working of selected Mahila Mandals in the states of Gujarat, Jammu and Kashmir, Orissa, Punjab and Tamil Nadu made clear that only a negligible proportion of women from the concerned villages had enrolled themselves as members of these organisations. According to the same study, attendance of the members from the lower castes and classes was significantly poor. Heading of these organisations was confined only to higher castes.[25]

The above need not necessarily lead to the conclusion that women's organisations, wherever they exist, are a failure. There are some Mahila Mandals whose efforts have been very beneficial to women. For example, the Badlao Foundation Mahila Mandal in Bihar put pressure on the Block Development Officer of that area to provide them with drinking water facilities and succeeded in getting the facilities. A Mahila Mandal in Bhagalpur, also in Bihar, could successfully persuade the local officials to establish a school.[26] Another important study connected with women and rural transformation also noticed the presence of successful Mahila Mandals.[27]

When once women's organisations are formed and become strong, they can influence their neighbourhoods and also function as powerful pressure groups for implementing the existing programmes and for introducing other needed ones.[28] Experts in social development and social change have noted that where women'sorganisations are active, changes are introduced quickly and their momentum maintained easily.[29] In addition to this, organisations facilitate and promote leadership.

Rural Women and Officials

The success of development programmes would depend largely upon the spirit of mutual understanding, harmony and cooperation between the public and official. With the introduction of Panchayati Raj, a number of officers like Block Development Officer, Mukhya Sevika, Gram Sevika have come into existence. The Mukhya Sevikas and Gram Sevikas are especially meant to work for the development of women. It would now be worthwhile to discuss the nature of relationship between the Panchayati Raj officials and women of rural areas. The Panchayati Raj officials could broadly be divided into three categories: top level, middle level and lower level officials. Collectors, District Development Officers and Block Development Officers come in the first category. The second category includes the Extension Officers in charge of health, education, social welfare and women welfare. The Mukhya Sevikas and the Gram Sevikas form part of the third category of officials.

Available evidence suggests that bureaucracy in general seems to concentrate more on programmes of general welfare and pay less attention to the programmes meant for weaker sections. And the programmes meant for women welfare receive even lesser attention than the programmes for weaker sections. It is also to be noted that the economically and socially privileged sections of society could get greater attention of the bureaucrats.[30] A study of rural women in Karnataka found that rural women feel that officials, with few exceptions, are corrupt and did not want to pass on the benefits earmarked for the poor. Some women in this State reported to the investigator that the officials claimed a big share in every benefit given to the poor and very often joined hands with the local landlords in harassing poor women. They also said that they found it difficult to get their grievances ventilated when the officials, who were expected to help the women, themselves take sides with the landlords.[31]

In the case of Andhra Pradesh, however, one study found that greater rapport between officials and public at various levels and men were also advised by officials to realise the need for involving women in developmental activities. This is what exactly is desired by the founders of Panchayati Raj and is true in some places. But it is too sanguine to expect the same situation in all places and at all times. The writer herself noticed an atmosphere of distrust existing between officials and women in some villages.

The nature of interaction of women officials and women in villages does not show a uniform pattern. The findings of a high power bureaucratic study team called The Rama Murthy Study Team which conducted studies in States like Andhra Pradesh, Uttar Pradesh, Maharashtra and Gujarat proved that women were critical of women officials, women did not possess initiative to communicate their problems to officials and women did not repose faith in the ability of women officials. But evidence to the opposite is also available. In some villages of Andhra Pradesh women are seen anxiously waiting for the arrival of Extension Officers for Women Welfare and Gram Sevikas to get the benefit of the programmes, especially income generating programmes meant for women. This particular group of women are those who are poor and who are engaged in non-agricultural activities like preparation of food products. This point needs elaboration. In fact in the element of lack of trust, there is implied a subtle disrespect towards these lower level women bureaucrats — disrespect partly based on suspicion about their gregarious behaviour, particularly their constant interaction with men. Rural values and norms of morality oppose women's intermingling with men and those who have to do this constantly are held disrespectful and interaction with such women is held undesirable. Such an atmosphere coupled with inadequate attention paid by rural institutions towards women welfare would not give scope for a proper utilization of the means for women's welfare. The writer had noticed that the meagre amounts meant for women welfare in a Samithi were left unspent for several years and surprisingly even during the period of a woman functioning as the President of that particular Samithi. It may not be irrelevant to point out that the records or diaries maintained by some officials are misleading. They show that they visited several places and in fact, not many of the places had been actually visited.

Strangely enough it is not always the case that official sections put on haughty airs and an attitude of talking down to the women target groups. There are instances of rich and middle segments of rural women adopting airs vis-a-vis lower level officials.

Impediments

It would now be worthwhile to note some important impediments for the development of rural women. Rural women in India suffer from several cultural constraints, though one can notice some degree of relaxation of these in recent times. Tradition in rural society inhibits women, particularly high caste and orthodox women, from playing active roles in the socio-economic process. Low level literacy ignorance, superstition, poverty, lack of time due to breadearning activities, which mainly include agricultural activity with low payments and absence of motivation, are some other bottlenecks for rural women's development.

In addition to the above, exploitation of women both within and outside the family, absence of proper motivation in the personnel connected with programme implementation, and inadequate political will at all levels of administration come in the way of success that could be achieved.

If the above are constraints for women's participation in the social and economic activity, the impediments for women's entry and participation in public life are many more. These would be discussed at relevant places in the following pages.

Do they all suggest that the future of Indian women in general and rural women in particular is dark? An examination of the situation in the right perspective and an optimistic assessment would definitely indicate the possibility of a better tomorrow. Some recent trends reveal that women are coming to the fore-front to take active roles in the socio-economic development and to assume leadership roles of political bodies also. One study on Women's Development Programmes in Rajasthan says that the introduction and implementation of these progammes from 1984 brought about significant changes in the pattern of social relationship. This study pointed out that the emerging pattern of social relationships is really challenging because of the growing consciousness among women relating to their participation in the planning process.[32] The emphasis given to women's development in the Sixth and Seventh Plans, introduction of schemes especially meant for women, the success of DWCRA scheme, legislation ensuring specific percentage of seats to women in the Panchayati Raj bodies in States like Andhra Pradesh and Karnataka, reservation of key positions to women in these institutions in the State of Andhra Pradesh, and finally the proposed Constitutional Amendment ensuring 30% of seats to women in the Panchayati Raj institutions are indicators of a hopeful situation.

References

1. Government of India, Committee on Plan Projects, Report of the Team for the Study of Community Projects and National Extension Service, 1957, Vol. I, p. 47.
2. *Ibid,* pp. 45-52.
3. *Ibid.*
4. Government of India, Report of the Committee on Panchayati Raj Institutions, 1978, pp. 141-142.
5. Government of India, Ministry of Human Resource Development, Dept. of Women & Child Welfare, National Perspective Plan for Women 1988-2000 A.D., Report of the Core Group, Akashdeep Printers, New Delhi, 1988, p. 4.
6. Source: Women & Development — Chapter in Sixth Five Year Plan — 1980-85, in *Handbook of Policy and Related Documents on Women in India,* National Institute of Public Co-operation and Child Development, New Delhi, 1988, pp. 63-68.
7. Seventh Five Year Plan — 1985-90: Socio-Economic Programme for Women, Chapter 17, Government of India, Planning Documents on Women in India, *op. cit.*, pp. 72-80.
8. *Ibid.*
9. Source: Government of India, Dept. of Rural Development, Ministry of Agriculture, Annual Report: 1987-88.
10. Indu Mathur, *Women and Social Change in Rajasthan,* Status of Women (ed) Susheela Agarwal, Printwell Publishers, Jaipur, p. 96.
11. Whyte Robert Orr and Pauline Whyte, *The Women of Rural Asia,* West-View Press, Boulder, Colorado, USA, 1982, p. 137.
12. Shramshakti: Report of the National Commission on Self-Employed Women and Women in the Informal Sector, June 1988, in *Handbook of Policy and Related Documents on Women in India, op. cit.* p. 97.
13. National Perspective Plan for Women, *op. cit. p. 6.*
14. Sumangala R., IRDP and Development of Rural Women in Subramanian R (ed), Rual Development: An Inside Look at Problems and Prospects, Yatan Publications, New Delhi, 1988, p. 102.
15. Government of India, Ministry of Human Resource Development, Dept. of Women and Child Welfare, National Perspective Plan for Women, 1988-2000 A.D., Report of the Core Group, Akashdeep Printers, New Delhi, 1988, p. 7.
16. Ranjana Kumari, *Women Headed Households in Rural India,* Radiant

Publishers, New Delhi, 1989, pp. 95-97.

17. Sarala Gopalam, *Why are Women Lagging Behind?*, Kurukshetra, Dec. 1987, p. 34.
18. Nalini Naik, Technology Change, the Labour Process and Employment in Relation to Women in the Fishing Sector, A Paper presented at the IV National Conference on Women's Studies, Waltair, Andhra Pradesh, 1988, p. 8 (unpublished).
19. Sarala Gopalam, *op. cit.*
20. Radha Paul, Women's Leadership in Welfare Work, *Social Welfare*, Vol. XXVII, No. 3, June 1980, pp. 4-5.
21. Secretary General, United Nations Organisation, Participation of Women in Community Development: Report of the Commission on the Status of Women, New York, 1972, pp. 23-57.
22. National Perspective Plan for Women, *op. cit.* p. 13.
23. Tak, B. L., *Sociological Dimensions of Gram Raj*, Vimal Prakashan, Ghaziabad, 1973, p. 148.
24. Martha F Loufti, Rural Women: Unequal Partners in Development, International Labour Office, Geneva, 1982, p. 74.
25. Jain, S. P. and V. Krishnamurty Reddy, *Role of Women in Development:* A Study of Mahila Mandals, National Institute of Rural Development, Hyderabad, 1979, p. 85.
26. Gautam Vohra, *Women in Bihar: A Study of the Role in Tassar Silk Production*, Vikas Publishing House, New Delhi, 1988.
27. Rekha Mehra and K. Saradamoni, *Women and Rural Transformation*, Concept Publishing House, New Delhi, 1982, pp. 24-25.
28. See: *Seminar*, May 1973. Special Number on the Status of Women.
29. United Nations Organisation, Report of the Secretary General, Participation of Women in Community Development, New York, 1972, p. 11.
30. Mumtaz Ali Khan, *Panchayati Raj and Weaker Sections of the Society:* Role of Village Panchayats (Summary of Proceedings of the Panchayati Raj Zonal Conference of Southern States held in 1976 in Bangalore and All India Panchayat Parishad, Delhi) p. 58.
31. Rao, U. N. J., *Women in a Developing Society*, Ashish Publishing House, New Delhi, 1985, p. 151.
32. Sharada Jain, Mamta Jaitly, Kavita Srivastava, Nirmala Nair and Kanchan Mathur, *Exploiting Possibilities: A Review of Women's Development Programme*, Rajasthan, Institute of Development Studies, Jaipur, 1988, p. 7.

3

Panchayati Raj Structures in India and Women's Representation

THE Panchayati Raj system in India is aimed at mobilising the effective participation of rural public in decision-making and in the implementation of rural welfare programmes. With this as the objective, efforts have been made to democratise the local institutions in India and to endow them with powers and authority to function as units of self-government. Care is taken to reserve certain number of seats to Scheduled Castes, Scheduled Tribes, Backward Classes and Minorities to provide representation to weaker sections. Special care is also taken to ensure representation of women in the Panchayati Raj structures.

Structures of Panchayati Raj[1]

The Panchayati Raj system in the country is generally a three-tier arrangement. The first tier at the village level is generally known as Gram Panchayat or Gaon Panchayat. The second[2] tier at the Block level, the constitution of which was suggested for the first time by the Balwantrai Mehta Committee, is generally known as the Panchayat Samithi. In the scheme suggested by this Committee, the Panchayat Samithi should be the most important body. The Committee opined that this body should act as an agent of the State Government in the execution of special schemes of development. The institution at the Block level is called Taluq Panchayat in Gujarat, Taluq Development Board in Karnataka, Janpad Panchayat in Madhya Pradesh, Panchayat Union in Tamil Nadu, Kshetra Samithi in Uttar Pradesh, Anchal Samithi in Arunachal Pradesh and Mandala Praja Parishad in Andhra Pradesh. The tier at the district or top level is generally called Zilla or District Panchayat. The Balwantrai Mehta Committee suggested that the Zilla Panchayat or Zilla Parishad should only be a coordinating body. In Assam, the district level body is known as Mohkuma Parishad. In the States of Tamil Nadu and Tripura it is called the District Development Council. In Andhra Pradesh, it is now designated as Zilla Praja Parishad.

Number of Tiers in States

Though the Balwantrai Mehta Committee suggested a three-tier system of Panchayati Raj, the number of tiers is determined by States themselves. This means that there is no uniformity in the matter of the number of units of local government in the Indian States and Union Territories. States and Union Territories having only a single tier-system include Jammu & Kashmir, Kerala, Tripura, Andaman and Nicobar Islands, Sikkim, Goa, Daman & Diu, Dadra and Nagar Haveli, Pondicherry and Delhi. The States with a two tier system are Assam, Haryana, Orissa and Manipur.

The three-tier system of Panchayati Raj, i.e. Gram Panchayat at village level, Panchayat Samithi at Block level, and Zilla Parishad at district level is in existence in Bihar, Gujarat, Himachal Pradesh, Madhya Pradesh, Maharashtra, Punjab, Rajasthan, Tamil Nadu, Uttar Pradesh, West Bengal, Arunachal Pradesh and Chandigarh. In Andhra Pradesh, the three-tiers are at Village, Mandal and District levels. In Karnataka they are at Mandal, Taluq and District levels. It should be noted here that a Mandal in Andhra Pradesh is a middle level unit and in Karnataka is the bottom level unit in Panchayati Raj. In Gujarat, Karnataka and Maharashtra, the second or the middle tier is at Taluq level. In Tamil Nadu, the third tier is at development district level instead of administrative district level.

Composition

The composition of Panchayati Raj structures at different levels in Indian States and Union Territories is the following:

District Level Bodies

The presiding officers of the Panchayati Raj structures below the level of Zilla Parishads become the members of Zilla Parishads. In the Panchayati Raj Acts of different States, care is taken to reserve some seats to Scheduled Castes and Scheduled Tribes. In Gujarat and Maharashtra, reservation to these sections is made on population basis. The minimum number of seats to be given to these sections is specified in the relevant Acts in the States of Andhra Pradesh, Assam, Bihar, Himachal Pradesh, Karnataka, Madhya Pradesh, Rajasthan and Uttar Pradesh and West Bengal.

The chairmen of these bodies are, in general indirectly elected. In

Andhra Pradesh, provision is made since 1987 for the direct election of the Chairman. In Arunachal Pradesh, the Chairman is nominated. In Tamil Nadu and Nagaland, the District Collector becomes the Chairman of the District Development Council. In the State of Andhra Pradesh, certain percentage of chairman's positions is reserved for Scheduled Castes and Scheduled Tribes, Backward Castes and women. It is very important to mention that in none of the States except in Andhra Pradesh, Chairmanship of Zilla Parishad is reserved for women. In all the States except in Maharashtra, the Members of Legislative Assembly, Legislative Council (if Council exists) and Parliament become ex-officio members.

In all the States except Nagaland and Punjab, certain percentage of seats is earmarked for women.

Middle Level Bodies

The Chairmen of the structures below the middle level bodies are memebrs of these institutions, whatever be the name given to them. Some seats are reserved on the basis of population to Scheduled Castes and Scheduled Tribes in the States of Gujarat, Maharashtra and Karnataka. The minimum number of seats to be provided for Scheduled Castes and Scheduled Tribes is specified in the relevant Acts in Andhra Pradesh, Bihar, Haryana, Himachal Pradesh, Madhya Pradesh, Orissa, Punjab, Rajasthan, Tamil Nadu and Uttar Pradesh. In all the States except Maharashtra, Members of Legislative Assembly, Legislative Council (if the State has a Council) and Parliament are members in these bodies. In all the States except in Andhra Pradesh, reservation of seats for women is guaranteed.

In the States of Andhra Pradesh and Madhya Pradesh certain percentage of chairmanship is reserved for Scheduled Castes and Scheduled Tribes. A significant feature of far-reaching benefit in Andhra Pradesh is that certain percentage of chair positions is reserved for women, the details of which would be dealt within the Chapter 5 'Woman Presiding Officers.'

Lower Level Bodies

The members of the lower level bodies, in all the States and Union Territories are directly elected. Reservation of seats to Scheduled Castes and Scheduled Tribes is a common feature with the exception of West Bengal where the State Government exercises the power of nominating members of these sections in these institutions.

As regards the election of Chairmen, direct election is introduced in all the States/Union Territories except in Jammu and Kashmir, Karnataka, Kerala, Madhya Pradesh, Maharashtra, Tripura, Uttar Pradesh and Andaman & Nicobar Islands.

In the matter of reserving Chairman's positions in Andhra Pradesh, reservation for Scheduled Castes and Scheduled Tribes is provided on population criterion. In no State including Andhra Pradesh presiding officers' positions of Gram Panchayats are reserved for women.

Tenure

The tenure of the Panchayati Raj bodies ranges from 3 years to 6 years. For example, in Arunachal Pradesh and Rajasthan, members of lower level bodies hold office for 3 years. In Assam and West Bengal, their tenure is 4 years and in Andhra Pradesh, 5 years. In Maharashtra the members of Gram Panchayats and district level bodies would be elected for 5 years and 6 years respectively.

Representation to Scheduled Castes, Scheduled Tribes, Backward Classes and Minorities, is ensured either by reserving specific constituencies or by nomination or by cooption. In the case of women also this practice is being followed. The recent trend is one of anti-cooption and pro-reservation. The argument against cooption is that the coopted members would be treated as second rate or class members by the elected representatives and this attitudinal constraint hampers purposeful participation.

The Proposed Constitutional Amendment

The inadequacies existing in the Panchayati Raj system have led to the realisation by the Government at the Centre of the need to introduce structural and functional changes in the set up. The failure to hold regular and periodical elections to the Panchayati Raj bodies, prolonged supersessions, inadequate representation to the weaker sections like the Scheduled Castes, Scheduled Tribes and women, lack of financial resources and inadequate devolution of powers and responsibilities to the Panchayati Raj institutions have received the special attention of the Central Government.[2] Having been deeply concerned with the inadequacies and with a view to preventing them, this government proposed to add a new part to the constitution, which part would be related to Panchayats. The result is the introduction of the Constitution (Sixty-fourth Amendment) Bill, 1989, on May 15th, 1989 by the Prime Minister himself. The objectives and contents of the Bill have now received nation-wide interest and are being extensively discussed.

The proposed amendment makes it obligatory to all States to establish a three-tier system of panchayats at the village, intermediate and district levels. But States having a population of less than 20 lakhs would not be obliged to establish Panchayats at the intermediate level. It is proposed to fill all seats in Panchayats at all levels by direct election. However, Members of the House of the People and of the Legislative Assembly and Chairpersons of Panchayats at the immediately lower level could be provided represntation without voting right.

The amendment also proposes to ensure a fixed tenure of 5 years for panchayats, provide for the constitution of Finance Commissions in the States to review the finances of the panchayats, vest in the Election Commission the superintendence, direction and control of elections to the panchayats and empower the Comptroller and Auditor General of India to cause the accounts of panchayats audited.

The Constitution Amendment Bill is also particularly concerned with ensuring due representation to the Scheduled Castes, Scheduled Tribes and Women. 30% of the seats reserved for the Scheduled Castes and the Scheduled Tribes shall be reserved for women belonging to these communities. It is further provided that 30% of the total number of seats in the Panchayati Raj bodies should be reserved for women. However, this 30% includes the number of seats reserved for Scheduled Castes or Scheduled Tribes women as the case may be. The number of seats reserved for women will be allotted by rotation to different constituencies in a Panchayat. The State Governments are left with the option of providing or not for the reservation of the office of chairpersons for Scheduled Castes, Scheduled Tribes and women.[3]

The proposed Constitution Amendment is important in some respects. By making the three-tier system obligatory for the States to adopt, it provides for a more uniform pattern. The introduction of direct election to all the seats in the Panchayati Raj bodies, gives to the system a more democratic character. The decision of the Government to provide 30% reservation to women is commendable. But one has to admit that providing 30% reservation is not all that dramatic as it may sound because in States like Andhra Pradesh and Karnataka reservation up to 25% is already existing.

The Amendment would certainly bring about increased influence, if not control, of the Centre over Gram Raj. The successful implementation of the spirit of the Amendment depends largely on the political will of the leaders.

Women in the Panchayati Raj Structures

From the above, it is clear that the Acts governing political bodies in rural India are particular that women should find compulsory representation in these bodies and in general, care is taken to ensure women's presence in these bodies. For a clearer understanding of this, a study of the details of the position existing in some States would be useful.

Andhra Pradesh

Andhra Pradesh is one of the few States to introduce the Panchayati Raj set up as early as 1959. These Panchayati Raj institutions in Andhra Pradesh are known as Zilla Praja Parishads (these are set up at the district level and were known as Zilla Parishads), Mandala Praja Parishads (formerly called Panchayat Samithi) and Gram Panchayats. The present Mandala Praja Parishads, the middle level bodies are smaller units than the former Panchayat Samithis and the Mandala Praja Parishads are organised with the hope of 'coming nearer the door steps of the rural public'. It will be useful to explain the position in the ascending order starting from the Gram Panchayats.

The composition and functions of the Gram Panchayats in Andhra Pradesh are governed by the Andhra Pradesh Gram Panchayats Act, 1964 as amended till date. This Act provides for reservation of two seats for women if the total strength of the Gram Panchayat is 9 or less, 3 seats if the strength is between 10 and 15 and 4 seats if the strength is more than 15.[4] It is clear that the Act ensured between 22 to 25 per cent representation to women in these bodies. The presence of women in these bodies is necessary not only to give them a status in political institutions but also to know their views and use their talent. The objectives of Integral Rural Development could not be achieved without reasonable representation to women in these bodies.

In the middle level bodies, till, 1986, women's representation was governed by the Andhra Pradesh Panchayat Samithis and Zilla Parishads Act and since 1986 by the Andhra Pradesh Mandala Praja Parishads, Zilla Praja Parishads and Zilla Pranalika Abhivrudhi Sameeksha Mandals Act as amended by Act 3 of 1987. The Andhra Pradesh Panchyat Samithis and Zilla Parishads Act provided for cooption of two women for each Samithi in addition to the possibility of women members finding membership in Panchayat Samithis through the electoral process.[5] An amendment to the Act in 1963 specifically stated that there should be a standing committee of 7 members called Committee for Women Welfare which will also be incharge of Child Welfare in each Samithi and that a majority of members on this Committee should be women.[6] This Amendment Act also provided that on the Standing Committee for Education, at least one woman representative should be there. But the Committee on Women Welfare met with a strange fate when it got amalgamated, in 1976, with the Committee for Social Welfare. Thus the Committee on Women Welfare which had a majority of women on it got eclipsed. The reasons for this were as expected. These standing committees in many cases proved to be very ineffective and inactive. Even enlisting women in these committees became a problem at the

Samithi and Zilla Parishad levels.

The provisions relating to representation for women on Zilla Parishads and their standing committees were similar to those concerning Panchayat Samithis.

As mentioned before, women's representation in the middle and district level bodies is now governed by the Andhra Pradesh Mandala Praja Parishads, Zilla Praja Parishads and Zilla Pranalika Abhivrudhi Sameeksha Mandals Act, 1986. This Act is important in three respects in the present context. It guarantees representation to women in Zilla Parishads as it provides reservation of 9% of the total number of officers of Chairmen of Zilla Praja Parishads and Presidents of Mandala Praja Parishads to women.[7] Thus the Act can be hailed as an important measure in the context of ensuring some percentage of key positions to women. The Act is also important because it has reconstituted the Standing Committee for Women Welfare. The Act emphasises that a majority of memebrs of this committee should be women.

An examination of the provisions relating to women's representation in the above mentioned Act makes clear that proper thinking has not gone into the matter of integrating women into the representative and leadership roles. At the lowest level, the principle of reservation has been applied only in respect of women's membership in Gram Panchayats but not to the offices of Sarpanch. A more important lacuna is that representation to women in the middle level bodies namely, the Mandala Praja Parishads is not guaranteed. Under the existing system, it is only those women who could successfully contest along with others for the posts of Sarpanch that would become members of Mandala Praja Parishads.[9] In the elections in Andhra Pradesh to Gram Panchayats in 1987, about only 100 women contested for the office of Sarpanch while the number of offices is as much as 19,517. As the position stands, the Mandala Praja Parishads suffer from under-representation of women in them.

Karnataka

The State of Karnataka has made provisions for including women in the political institutions of Panchayati Raj. The Act governing Gram Panchayats indicates that at least two seats should be reserved for women in each Village Panchayat.

The Government has introduced additional structures in the Panchayati Raj set up by an Act in 1983, known as the Karnataka Zilla Parishads, Taluka Panchayat Samithis, Mandala Panchayats and Nyaya Panchayats Act, 1983. The two-tier system which the State had practiced till recently has been replaced by a three-tier system. It would now be worthwhile to consider the details relating to women's representation in this Act. In the Mandala Praja Parishads (which did not exist earlier) 25% of the total number of seats should be reserved for women.[10] The Act is also particular that out of the 25% of seats so reserved, one seat should be reserved for a woman belonging to Scheduled Castes or Scheduled Tribes.[11] The Act further says that on the Social Justice Committee (which can be regarded the counter part of the Committee on Women Welfare existing in Andhra Pradesh) which exists both at the Mandal as well as Zilla Parishad levels, at least one woman should find place. This Committee would be in charge of securing social justice to Scheduled Castes, Scheduled Tribes, women and other weaker sections of society.

One of the very important features of the Act is that it ensures representation to women in Nyaya Panchayats functioning at the Mandal level. The Nyaya Panchayat is a judicial body of five members and in this important institution, at least one member should be a woman,[12] the Act specifies.

The Act also makes clear that 25% of the seats should be reserved for women in the Zilla Parishads constituted at the district level. Representation for women in the Social Justice Committee, at the district level, is ensured.

A careful study of the Karnataka Acts relating to Panchayati Raj structures reveals that the framers have realised the need for women's representation at all levels. But the point is that at none of the levels, reservations for the offices of Chairman have been provided for.

Haryana

In the State of Haryana, there is provision for the cooption of one woman member to the Gram Panchayat, of one or two woman members to the Panchayat Samithi and of two woman members to the Zilla Parishad.[13]

Madhya Pradesh

The Panchayat legislation in this State provides for a minimum representation of two women in these local bodies at village and block levels and one at the district level whenever necessary by means of cooption.[14]

Maharashtra

The Acts governing Maharashtra Panchayati Raj institutions provide for the reservation of two seats for women at the Gram Panchayat level. At the Panchayat Samithi level, cooption of one woman member (if women are not elected) is to be made. In the case of Zilla Parishad, two woman members are to be coopted if the directly elected members do not include women.[15]

Punjab

The structural frame of Panchayati Raj in Punjab is also a three-tier one consisting of Gram Panchayats, Panchayat Samithis and the Zilla Parishads. The working of the Panchayati Raj institutions in the State is governed by the Punjab Gram Panchayats Act, 1952 and the Punjab Panchayat Samithis and Zilla Parishads Act, 1961.

The Punjab Gram Panchayat Act says that in every Panchayat there should at least be two women members. The Act does not provide for reservation of seats for women, but makes provision for the inclusion of unsuccessful women in this body if it does not consist of successful women candidates. If there are no women contestants in the election, women's representation should be ensured by means of cooption.[16]

There should be two women members in each Panchayat Samithi and two women members in each Zilla Parishad. The principle of cooption is to be adopted if these bodies do not already have woman membership in them.[17] Thus cooption is accepted as a last resort measure.

Rajasthan

Rajasthan Government's Gram Panchayats Act of 1953 and the Panchayat Samithis and Zilla Parishads Act of 1959 govern the constitution of the Panchayati Raj bodies in the State. The Panchayat Samithis and the Zilla Parishads Act provides that two women should be coopted to Panchayat Samithi if no woman is a member of Panchayat Samithi and only one, if a woman is already its member. Similar provision is included in the Act as regards women's representation in the Zilla Parishads.

Tamil Nadu

Women's representation in the Panchayati Raj bodies of Tamil Nadu is governed by the Tamil Nadu Panchayats Act, 1958 as amended up-to-date. As pointed out earlier, the lower level panchayat structures in this State are called the Village and Town Panchayats, and the intermediary level structures are called Panchayat Union Councils. At the apex are the District Development Councils.

The Act provides for reservation of one seat for women in the Village and Town Panchayats.[18]

The Panchayat Union Council consists of the Chairman, Presidents of all Panchayats in the Panchayat Union, one non-official member of each township committee in the Panchayat Union, coopted members and the nominated members. The Act is particular that in the Panchayat Union Councils representing Panchayats not exceeding 12 in number, at least 2 women should find representation. In the

Panchayat Union Councils consisting of 13 to 20 Panchayats, at least 3 women representatives should be there. In the Panchayat Union Councils representing more than 20 Panchayats, 5 women members should be included.[19] Thus more than proportionate increase in women's representation is ensured as the middle level body gets bigger. The principles of election, nomination and cooption could be used to ensure women's representation on these bodies. It is the people who will have a say in the election of women members. The Collector is empowered to nominate women members[20] and it is the Councils that exercise the power of cooption. The final outcome as envisaged by the Act is that of ensuring the specified representation to women. One important point that deserves special attention in this context is that the Act disqualifies the wife or the husband of a member of a panchayat union to become coopted members.[21] Persons who do not have aptitude for rural development are also barred from becoming nominated members.[22] The inclusion of these provisions could be supported on the ground that the representatives of Panchayati Raj bodies should consist of really 'rural development oriented' and not 'Yes Persons' and that necessary legal provisions to this effect should be provided for. But disqualifying citizens on grounds of family relationships is not only unconstitutional but also morally unjustifiable. The possibility of constructive roles of family members by becoming members could not be ruled out.

The above discussion gives an understanding of statutory position regarding women's representation and sets the stage for an examination of the participatory position.

References

1. The sources of information relating to the Panchayati Raj structures are the following:
   (a) *Panchayati Raj at a Glance: Status of Panchayati Raj Institutions in India*, 1987-88, Government of India, Ministry of Agriculture, Department of Rural Development, Administrative Intelligence Division, Krishi Bhavan, New Delhi, Jan. 1989.
   (b) The Andhra Pradesh Mandala Praja Parishads, Zilla Praja Parishads and Zilla Pranalika Abhivrudhi Sameeksha Mandals Act, 1986 as amended by Act 3 of 1987, Asia Law House, Hyderabad, 1987. See the statement of objects and reasons.
2. The Constitution (Sixty-Fourth Amendment) Bill, 1989.
3. The Constitution (Sixty-Fourth Amendment) Bill, 1989, Provisions 243-243M.
4. Section 9, 3(a), the Andhra Pradesh Gram Panchayats Act, 1964 as amended till date.

5. Section 4, Sub-section 1, clause V(a), the Andhra Pradesh Panchayat Samithis and Zilla Parishads Act, 1959.
6. Section 14, Sub-section 3, The Andhra Pradesh Panchayat Samithis and Zilla Parishads Act, 1959 as amended in 1964.
7. Section 5, Sub-section 2 (b), The Andhra Pradesh Mandala Praja Parishads, Zilla Praja Parishads and Zilla Pranalika Abhivrudhi Sameeksha Mandals Act, 1986 as amended by Act 3 of 1987.
8. *Ibid*, Section 51(iv) and 51, 2 (b).
9. Each Mandala Praja Parishad consists of a directly elected President, Sarpanches of the Gram Panchayat in the Mandal, Members of the Legislative Assembly of the State representing a constituency which comprises the Mandal, Member of the House of the People representing the constituency which comprises the Mandal, Member of the Council of States, if any from the area and a representative of minorities.
10. Section 5(2), The Karanataka Zilla Praja Parishads, Taluka Panchayat Samithis, Mandala Panchayats and Nyaya Panchayats Act, 1983.
11. *Ibid.*
12. *Ibid.*
13. Source: Hargian Singh, *Rural Political System in India*, Indira Publishers, Gurgaon, 1985, pp. 21-25.
14. Source: (a) *Women and Children in Madhya Pradesh : A Profile*, Mahila Chetna Manch, Bhopal, 1985, p. xxxiv.

    (b) Hazel D'Lima, *Women in Local Government : A Study of Maharashtra*, Concept Publishing Company, New Delhi, 1983, pp 18-19.
15. Source: Rajput, R.S. (ed) *Panchayati Raj in India : Democracy at Grass Roots*, Deep and Deep Publications, New Delhi, 1984, pp. 137-140.
16. Section 6, Punjab Gram Panchayat Act, 1952 as amended up-to-date.
17. Section 5 and 86, the Punjab Panchayat Samithis and Zilla Parishads Act, 1961.
18. Section 15(3), The Tamil Nadu Panchayats Act, 1958.
19. Section 12, *Ibid.*
20. Section 12(1-A) ii, 1B (ii) and 1 (c) ii. *Ibid.*
21. Section 12 (c) ii. *Ibid.*
22. *Ibid.*

4

The Participatory Position

THE preceding discussion provides the background for an examination of the role of women in the Panchayati Raj institutions which are the centres of decision-making in the rural scene. In fact, as pointed out in the National Perspective Plan for Women, "political power and access to positions of decision-making and authority are critical pre-requisites for women's equality in the process of nation building."[1] Participation in the Panchayati Raj institutions, in the present context includes attendance in membership and participation in the committees of these bodies; moving resolutions; taking part in discussions; participation in the final point of decision-making and the follow-up activity of observing how far the decisions of these institutions are implemented.

Available evidence on the role of women in Panchayati Raj bodies enables one to identify the basic pattern running throughout the system. The selection process and the quality of membership, awareness and instutional participation would be the main points for discussion in this chapter.

Selection Process and Quality of Membership

Participation whether it be in the political process or political institutions requires involvement, cooperation, knowledge, contribution and follow-up action. Participation and quality of membership are closely related, and quality in its turn depends on the process of selection.

Women could get into the rural political institutions through open competition, by contesting the reserved seats, by means of cooption and by the method of nomination. As is well known, the chances of women entering these institutions by way of open competition are very limited in our country. Definitely talented and capable women can contest, be nominated or coopted to these bodies and can contribute their mite to rural reconstruction. But in a large number of cases, caste and familial or social nearness to the president (of a panchayat body) have been given greatest importance in the recruitment of women.[2] The writer has come across several such instances during her field work. In one village, the mother of the Sarpanch was one of the two women representatives of the Gram Panchayat and the other was the wife of a close associate of the Sarpanch. It is surprising that the Sarpanch's mother was totally unaware of the fact that she represented women on the Panchayat. She could only recollect that her son occasionally asked her to put her thumb impression in a book. In another village, some women have been elected for successive terms and the only activity that these women had been involved in the working of the Gram Panchayat is that of putting their thumb impression in the records when required.[3]

Experience in Andhra Pradesh in implementing the principle of cooption shows that, in general, women got coopted in a very perfunctorily manner without any thought being given to their experience, knowledge and ability.

The position in Karnataka is similar to that which exists in Andhra Pradesh. The polls in 1984 in Karnataka revealed that the women representatives have largely been relatives of men in power.[4]

While this is the position in general, there are some exceptions. In a village which is advanced in terms of per capita income, literacy rate, educational facilities, and nearness to national highways, the writer has come across a female representative who later became the Sarpanch of her village. She had been a very active participant and the chief factors that contributed to this had been husband's support, personal interest and commitment to development.

Awareness

An examination of the levels of awareness of the members of any society would be of great use in analysing the nature and extent of their participation. Awareness and participation are closely related. Awareness tends to promote participation while participation in turn would certainly make the participant more politically aware. Thus there is a circularity syndrome inherent in the awareness-participation relationship. Awareness here is taken to mean knowledge of the needs of the people, functions of political institutions, their purposes and procedures and knowledge of one's own role in and outside the institutions and more importantly knowledge of the local bodies and environment.

It is difficult to make generalisations about awareness and equally difficult to assess the levels of awareness. But an attempt is made by the writer to find out the degree of awareness with the assistance of a set of questions in some places of Andhra Pradesh. It has been noticed that a majority of rural women are aware of their needs but not of the programmes for the development and the means to realise their needs. As regards awareness of members in general, the Samithis/Mandals have shown a better position than the villages and the Zilla Parishads/Zilla Praja Parishads than the Samithis/Mandals.

Mention should be made of the emerging trends in some villages of Andhra Pradesh. Around 20% of women have shown concern for improving women's lot and it must be said that this is a significant improvement over the years. An anxiety to get enlightened about the sources of achieving their objectives is also seen among these women who form a significant percentage of the total.

The awareness of the rural women of Karnataka according to the available evidence is the following. A majority of women is not aware of the importance of Village Panchayats and the degree of absence of awareness is more among the Muslims than the Hindus. This tallies with the general inference that religious minorities especially minorities like the Muslims tend to show lower levels of awareness. Women do not, also, in general, show awareness of the importance of Village Panchayats for the development of women. According to one study, 90% of women consider Village Panchayats as 'the worst organisations' and believe that they are not useful for the development of women.[5]

As regards the position in Maharashtra, one study points out that women are fairly progressive in outlook, ready to recognise the demands of a changing social situation and willing to participate in the socio-economic and political process.[6]

A study held on Women Leadership at the Grass Roots Level in Punjab has noted that most of the woman Panchs were neither aware of their role — their rights and duties nor the functioning of the Panchayats and that they are just satisfied with the prestige and status symbol of being a Panch. It is the lack of realisation of the importance of attending the meetings that led to their low level political participation. Some members said that they were never informed about the meetings. Some others said that they could not attend the meetings on account of illness. Few of them were frank enough in saying that they did not bother about the meetings.[7]

In West Bengal, political awareness of women, in general, was found to be of a fairly low level. But within the framework of a generally low level of awareness, rural women's awareness was less in degree than that of urban women.[8]

Institutional Participation

Participation in political institutions provides an important indicator for development because these are the centres of final decision making. In the absence of participation in these institutions, women at best become beneficiaries and not contributors to development. The participation of rural Indian women should be viewed in the background of generally prevailing constraints like ignorance, illiteracy, absence of awareness, motivation and traditional taboos. But it should also be borne in mind that a noticeable change has come over in the psychological and sociological dimensions in some parts of rural India and this should argue well for a better situation.

As regards women members attending the meetings, in Andhra Pradesh, the writer noticed in one of her studies a significant variation between the attendance records and actual attendance. The records make one think that all the members of Gram Panchayats had shown very high interest in attending the meetings. But the fact is that women members rarely attend meetings. Very often registers are sent to their homes for their signatures or thumb impressions. The difference between attendance in records and actual attendance is less significant in Samithis (Since 1987 Mandals). In the case of women members of Zilla Parishads, now Zilla Praja Parishads, the tendency of not attending meetings was more when compared to those of the Samithis. However, in her recent study, the writer found that the women members' interest in attending the meetings of Zilla Praja Parishad is significant.

The position in the matter of women members attending the meetings of the Panchayati Raj bodies in Haryana is equally unsatisfactory. As one study pointed out, the women members of Gram Panchayats rarely attend meetings. Women members of group or groups opposing the Sarpanchs will be discouraged by the male members of opposition with the objective of not facilitating quorum. In the case of coopted women members, if they happen to be the supporters of the Sarpanch, they are presumed to be present whether they are really present or not. In the case of Samithi and Zilla Parishad meetings, women members would be present but in purdah or under veil,[9] as is common in some parts of North India.

Evidence about Karnataka rural women's participation in the political institutions shows that they rarely attend the meetings. Even when they attend, they did not participate in the deliberations. In this context, the findings of a study[10] can be mentioned. It was noticed by the investigators of the study that women members found it difficult to attend meetings regularly because of their domestic preoccupations. Some members even said that they could not attend meetings because of the problem in walking long distances to reach the meeting places.

A study of the women members of some Panchayat Samithis in Maharashtra helps one to infer that as far as attendance is concerned, the situation is not unsatisfactory.[11] The finding of one study in

Punjab in respect of women members attending meetings of Gram Panchayats is that 53% of them never attended meetings and it was only 23.33% members that regularly attended.[12]

Vocal Participation

While attendance is a mark of physical participation, participation in moving resolutions, discussions, decision-making and follow-up action are indicators of vocal participation. It is difficult to assess the nature and extent of women's participation in these aspects precisely because of the fact that studies which lay emphasis on these matters are very limited in number. Most of the studies on rural women cover largely their role in socio-economic activity and only occasional mention of political activity is made in them. Even these references are very general in nature and point out that women members rarely or occasionally attend meetings and that they do not participate in them. This can be accepted as the general trend, no doubt. But it is possible to bring to light the real contribution of some women members, though few in number, with the assistance of micro-level studies. It is these women who become the models for aspiring leadership. Some important micro-level studies have been conducted in the States of Andhra Pradesh, Maharashtra and Punjab. The study in Andhra Pradesh was made by the writer and this examined the role of women members at all the three levels of Panchayati Raj structures. The Maharashtra study[13] which will be discussed in this chapter dealt with women's participatory position at the Panchayati Samithi and Zilla Parishad levels. The Punjab study[14] was concerned with the participation of women members at the Gram Panchayat level. These micro-level studies may not help to make generalisations, but would be of immense utility to serve as samples for future research. The following are the details.

Andhra Pradesh

Before dealing with the details of participation of women members as revealed by the study of writer, a brief explanation of the sample is necessary. The respondents include women members of all the three tiers. Care was taken to choose respondents from the ordinary and advance Samithis/Mandals as well as Gram Panchayats to facilitate comparisons of a meaningful nature. To identify the advanced and ordinary Samithis/Mandals and Gram Panchayats, the classification already made by the State Government in 1965 was adopted. The criteria fixed by the Government includes per-capita land revenue, percentage of irrigated area to cultivated area, percentage of children of the age group of 6-11 attending schools, literacy and communication.

The number of respondents in the sample is 88.

Initiating Resolutions

Initiating resolutions forms one of the imporant aspects of participatory process. This role requires cosiderable home-work and knowledge of the matters which form part of resolutions. It is also essential that one must have a clear knowledge of the purpose of the institutions and also the procedure through which decisions could be taken to realise the needs. As seen earlier, most of the women members are not aware of the purposes, functions and procedures of the so-called new Panchayati Raj institutions even after three decades of their emergence.

Coming to the sample, in the Gram Panchayat under study, four women moved resolutions. One was the Sarpanch of a Gram Panchayat. In the early period of her office, she could very easily secure the support of a majority of members for her resolutions. But factional politics in the village put her in a position of stress and strain and the consequent events actually led to the taking over of the administration of the village by a special officer appointed by the Government.

Another woman, a member of a Gram Panchayat who represents her ward since 1981 is the most active member of not only woman members but of the total membership of the Panchayat itself. In an interview on 7.6.1989, by the writer, this woman member said, "we are elected by the people and for the people. They (the people) have given us this respectable position. It is our duty to serve them and keep up the dignity and the status of our membership."

In the Samithis, as well as in the Zilla Parishad/Zilla Praja Parishad, the role of women members in moving resolutions is usually indirect. On requests made by women members, resolutions used to be moved in the meetings by male members, more often by the presiding officers.

One important development since 1987 is that the women members of the Zilla Parishad (who are the presidents of their respective Mandals Praja Parishads) give written representation to the presiding officers of Zilla Parishads and get the desired work done since these women are the presiding officers at the Mandal levels, and they do participate in the act of moving resolutions.

Discussions

Participatory democracy believes in the principle of arriving at decisions after proper deliberations. It is necessary that considerable time is given and opportunities made available for discussion by all the members to prevent monopoly of decision-making by a few. It was noticed that in this act of participation, the record of 86.66% women members in the Gram Panchayats is nil. The women members, presiding officers and the officials said that woman members' vocal participation in Gram Panchayats is limited. Mere observation and silence are the general characteristic features. A very curious example is that of a women member who innocently stated at the time of interview that "Does it not mean showing disrespect to the Sarpanch if I speak in the meeting?". It must be pointed out here that opportunities for participation in discussion whether for male or female members are totally foreclosed in some villages because of the fact that meetings of Gram Panchayats do not take place at all. The writer has come across instances when resolutions of Gram Panchayats are written in advance (by clerks on the directions of the Sarpanch) pending formal approval of the Gram Panchayat members by giving their signatures

While the above is the general trend, women members in advanced villages took part in discussions. As already pointed out, one woman Sarpanch of an advanced village was very active, persuasive and public spirited and she did considerable service to the village. Some of the recently elected women members of Gram Panchayats are quite active, have a comprehensive view of the needs of women as well as the villages and are active participants in discussions. The active and more active participants of woman members in Gram Panchayats constitute 13.33% and 6.66% respectively.

Panchayat Samithis & Mandala Praja Parishads

As pointed out earlier, the Panchayat Samithis were the intermediary bodies till 1987 and the Mandala Praja Parishads since then. In the Samithis, in general, 32.15% of the women members participated in discussions and some had in the absence of the President, even presided over the meetings of the Standing Committee on Women Welfare. One important point to be mentioned in connection with the functioning of the Committee on Women Welfare is that this Committee, on several occasions, delegated its powers either to the president or to the executive officer. This practice is defective in that it weakens the democratic institutions and defeats the very purpose of democratic decentralisation on the basis of which the Panchayati Raj bodies are organised. In the ordinary Samithi only 17.64% showed interest in discussions. Their only concern was women welfare and particularly establishment of sewing centres in their villages and were successful in their attempts.

Participation of woman members of advanced Samithi in discussions was found to be better than that in the ordinary Samithi. Here 46.67% of the women members showed interest in discussions.

Some women members could successfully persuade their co-members in getting benefits to their constituents. But the area of interest was confined to women welfare and even in this, only to the establishment of dress-making centres and Mahila Mandals and providing shelter to destitute women and orphans. Very few women participated in discussion regarding general welfare activities. The percentage of active women members in the advanced Samithis is 13.33%, though low, is not insignificant.

The participation of women members of the Mandala Praja Parishads is very encouraging. As mentioned already, except in the Mandala Praja Parishads where the chair-position is held by women, women are rarely present. But among those who took these positions, a good number of women, are found to be actively involved in their functions.

Zilla Parishads

The women members of Zilla Parishad showed a greater degree of participation, they are more active, better informed and better educated than the Samithi members. They are not only interested in Women Welfare Programmes but also in all the welfare programmes in general. More than 50% of them took reasonably good part in discussions relating to women welfare, communication, health, sanitation, schools and tribal welfare.

Decisions

The study revealed that women in key positions with interest and talent could play considerable role in the final point of decision-making. The participation of a majority of members of Gram Panchayats is nil in this aspect. But a significant percentage of 6.66 is very active.

For instance, a member of a Gram Panchayat, who is regular in attendance could get the decisions in favour of her proposals and provide for drainage, water, road, lighting and other facilities to her consitituents. With confidence, the woman member, G. Mariamma said that she derived satisfaction by securing the above facilities to her constituents. She also said that she would continuously persuade the officials for the implementation of the sanctioned works. It should be pointed out here that this member, belonging to lower middle class Christian family, and educated only upto 6th class is a real benefactor to the electors. This is mostly due to her dynamic personality. Her case offers a good example to prove that political power is not always shared and exercised by socially and economically dominant sections in the Panchayati Raj system.

In the Panchayat Samithis, it is through persuasion that women members could get favours done to their areas. The participation of some *ex-officio* member of Zilla Parishad is encouraging. A few of the coopted members also could convince their colleagues and get their proposals accepted by the Zilla Parishad. Some examples would now be useful to assess the role of women members in the discussions and decisions of the Zilla Parishad. Smt. K. Prabhavati, a Mahila Mandal President and a coopted member of the Zilla Parishad of the East Godavari District in Andhra Pradesh could convince the officials and non-officials that the establishment of a Mahila Mandal in the heart of the village would be more profitable than in the outskirts. She herself donated land in which the Mahila Mandal building was constructed. This Mahila Mandal has a very well-equipped library in terms of meeting the needs of village women and is engaged in various activities of women's interest. One woman President of a Samithi, Smt. B. Rajarajeswaramma, could get several welfare measures implemented in her Samithi. Some of the *ex-officio* members, Smt. N. Vijayalakshmi, Smt. Y. Savitri Devi, Smt. D. Bhanutilakam, Smt. G. Kamala Devi and Kumari T. Ratna Bai in their capacity as ex-officio members of the Zilla Parishad they represented could contribute fairly to their constituents. Their efforts led to improvement in communications, education, sanitation, health and irrigation. One of these *ex-officio* member, Smt. N. Vijayalakshmi had also held the position of Deputy Minister in-charge of Women Welfare for sometime. Kumari T. Ratna Bai who represented a tribal constituency during 1972-78 in the A.P. Legislative Assembly brought several developments in her constituency. The establishment of a Govt. Junior College, Integrated Tribal Development Agency, Agricultural Development Bank, Tribal Girls Hostel and Sub-treasury in Rampachodavaram, a town in one of the tribal areas in Andhra Pradesh. Construction of Pamuleru Bridge and Maddigadda Reservoir, construction of Ashram schools, upgrading of several schools and the development of communications—all in this area are her chief achievements.

Follow-up Action

The women members with the exception of one or two have not shown any interest in the follow-up action of observing the implementation of decisions.

Maharashtra

The details of institutional participation of women members according to the study in Maharashtra based on interviews with 144 members of some Zilla Parishads and Samithis are the following. The study found out high performers as well as low performers among women in these bodies. Women with secondary and high educational qualifications and political background, those who lived in places adjoining urban areas and belonged to well-to-do families, women who had membership in other associations and those who were exposed to the environment on account of travelling considerably were found to be high performers. The percentage of high performers, according to the study, is 25. The low performers were those who were poorly educated and illiterates, confined to rural set-up, having varying degrees of political influence and not able to leave their homes and travel.

Mention was made in the study of the involvement of women members in the activities of Mahila Mandals, bhajan groups, craft classes, adult education among women and welfare activities for children. They were also interested and involved in procuring basic amenities like drinking water, approach roads and agricultural inputs. They have also been successful in finding employment opportunities and financial assistance to the needy especially backward classes.

The above study further pointed out that a majority of rural women proved to be effective at grass-roots levels.

Another interesting finding of the study is that 43% of the women members of Zilla Parishads and Panchayat Samithis in the sample had experience in Village Panchayats and these women were found to be having great potential to work for the improvement of rural women's conditions. A majority of the respondents in the study expressed considerable satisfaction with their membership in these bodies mainly because of self-confidence and social awareness they derived from their participation. There was found a desire in all of them to meet the challenges of their new roles. For instance, they did not any longer find it difficult to travel alone, to sit in the meetings along with male members and freely express their views. Their membership in these bodies also helped them in giving less importance to caste considerations. Some important development trends of breaking away from traditional barriers, of stimulated interest in community work, and the development of leadership qualities and interest in areas beyond rural development were noticed among a good number of respondents.

Punjab

The study held in the Punjab on the basis of interviews with 30 women Panchas makes clear the following facts. The Panchas were passive members rather than agents of change. A majority of them had not attended the meetings and even those who attended did not have confidence to discuss various issues raised. One of he respondents remarked that it is not important that women should interfere in each and every matter discussed in the meetings. She further said that on certain issues, men have more wisdom than women.

Most of the women respondents positively responded to male domination in general and also in the context of panchayat bodies. Neither did they question nor ever resent this feature of the social system. Among the 30 respondents, it was only one woman (a graduate) who said that she had an argument with the Sarpanch whose action in one context was found wrong by her and she had also brought it to the notice of the officials. But such an action by women members would generally not be favourably received by the villagers who even go to the extent of spreading scandals about women members. In fact, vocal participation by women is generall associated with the women being regarded as permissive in their behaviour and as being even of loose character, according to another respondent in the sample. The situation is that requiring a dramatic change in the attitudinal aspect.

The above discussion helps one to conclude that some women of the rural areas in India proved themselves exceptional as representatives in political institutions. In the 70s and more so in the 80s women with considerable interest in improving women's lot and rural development entered these bodies. This is definitely a trend towards revitalisation.

References

1. Government of India, National Perspective Plan for Women, 1988-2000 AD, Report of the Core Group set up by the Department of Women and Child Development, Akashdeep Printers, New Delhi, 1988, p. 13.
2. See also (a) Sriranjani Subbarao K. Role of Women in the Panchayati Raj Institutions: A case study of Visakhapatanam Zilla Parishad, Kosimkota, Ravikantam and Madugula Mandala Praja Parishads and six Gram Panchayats, A paper presented at the IV National Conference on Women's Studies at Waltair, Andhra Pradesh, (unpublished) 1988, p.5 (b) Singh Hargian, *Rural Political System in India*, Indira Publishers, Gurgaon, 1985, pp. 21-25.
3. See also Chandramani, G.Y., Profiles of Women in Andhra Pradesh, Majumdar Vina (ed) *Symbols of Power*, Allied Publishers Pvt. Ltd., New Delhi, 1979, p. 189.
4. Amal Ray and Jayalakshmi Kumpatla, Zilla Parishad Presidents in Karnataka: Their Social Background and Implications for Development, *Economic and Political Weekly*, Oct. 17-24, 1984, pp. 18-26.
5. Mumtaz Ali Khan and Noor Ayesha, *Status of Rural Women in India: A Study of Karnataka*, Uppal Publishing House, New Delhi, 1987, pp. 113-114.

6. Hazel D'Lima, *Women in Local Government: A Study of Maharashtra*, Concept Publishing Company, New Delhi, 1983, p. 119.
7. Rajaput Pam, Women's Leadership at the Grass Roots Level in Punjab, A paper presnted at the Fourth National Conference on Women's Studies, Waltair, Andhra Pradesh, Dec.,1988, (unpublished), pp. 16-18.
8. Banerjee Nirmala, Politicization: Women in West Bengal, (ed) Vina Majumdar, *Symbols of Power, op. cit.* pp. 145-150.
9. Singh Hargian, *op. cit.*
10. Mumtaz Ali Khan and Noor Ayesha, *op.cit.* p. 134.
11. Hazel D'Lima, *op. cit.* p. 194.
12. Rajput Pam, *op. cit.* p. 17.
13. Hazel D'Lima, *op. cit.*
14. Rajput Pam, *op. cit.*

5

Focus on a Micro Setting

THE discussion in the previous chapter enables one to assess the nature and extent of participation of women members in general and those of some women members in particular in the Panchayati Raj bodies. The discussion also gives a detailed view of the position existing in the States of Andhra Pradesh, Maharashtra and Punjab. Some questions that consequently arise in this context are: (1) Who are the active participants and who are not? (2) What are the contributing factors for participation and active participation? (3) What is the relationship between background and recruitment as well as participation? Any attempt to answer these questions should be preceded by a micro-level examination of the socio-economic and political background of members and their impact on participation. In this chapter, a micro-level analysis of the socio-economic and political background of women members in the sample selected by the writer is detailed. The relationship between the background and participation is also assessed.

The Sample

Before dealing with the details, a word must be said about the sample. It consists of one Zilla Parishad, two Panchayat Samithis, five Mandala Praja Parishads and five Gram Panchayats. All these institutions with the exception of one Gram Panchayat in the Warangal district of Andhra Pradesh are selected from the East Godavari district which is one of the advanced districts in the State. As regards the two Panchayat Samithis selected for study, one is an ordinary Samithi and the other an advanced Samithi (the basis for the classification of Samithis into advanced and ordinary is already mentioned earlier). Two of the Gram Panchayats in the sample are advanced, two backward and one an All-Women Panchayat. The number of the members of Gram Panchayats, Mandala Praja Parishads, Panchayat Samithis and Zilla Parishad is 30, 5, 34, and 19 respectively. The socio-economic background of women members in the sample from 1956 to 1989 is studied with the help of the responses to an elaborate questionnaire with open ended and closed questions. The following are the details.

Gram Panchayats

In both the villages of the ordinary Samithi, there is no woman representative from the general seats. Only such number of women members as is required to be coopted or elected from the reserved seats, as the case may be, found representation on these Gram Panchayats. However, in the Panchayats of the advanced Samithi, the position is slightly different and better than that in the Gram Panchayats of the ordinary Samithi. The Gram Panchayat of the backward village in this Samithi had on the Gram Panchayat, a unanimously elected woman Sarpanch, elected in 1981. All the other women representatives were either coopted or elected from the reserved seats. The position is clear from Tables 5.1 & 5.1 (A). The basis for the division of the periods as shown in the Table can be explained. From 1956-1964, there was provision for cooption of women members to the Gram Panchayats. This provision was dispensed with from 1964. Hence the period from 1956-64 is taken as the first phase. Since 1964 elections to Gram Panchayats were held only four times, i.e. in 1964, 1970, 1981 and in 1987. However, in the advanced village of the ordinary Samithi, the members elected in 1981 continue to hold office till date as no elections were held in 1987 in this village.

TABLE 5.1
Women Member of Gram Panchayats
ORDINARY SAMITHI

Period	*Gram Panchayat of backward Village*			*Gram Panchayat of Advanced Village*		
	Required No. of women representatives	Actual No. of women representatives	Method of recruitment	Required No. of women representatives	Actual No. of women representatives	Method of recruitment
1956-64	1	1	Cooption	1	1	Cooption
1964-70	1	1	Election from reserved seats	2	2	Election from reserved seats
1970-81	1	1	"	2	2	"
1981-87	2	2	"	4	4	"
1987	2	2	"	4	4	"

TABLE 5.1(A)
Women Members of Gram Panchayats
ADVANCED SAMITHI

Period	*Gram Panchayat of Backward Village*			*Gram Panchayat of Advanced Village*		
	Required No. of women representatives	Actual No. of women representatives	Method of recruitment	Required No. of women representatives	Actual No. of women representatives	Method of recruitment
1956-64	1	1	Cooption	1	1	Cooption
1964-70	1	1	Election from reserved seats	2	2	Election from reserved seats
1970-81	1	1	"	2	2	"
1981-87	2	3	Election from reserved & unreserved seats	3	3	"
1987	2	2	Election from reserved seats	3	3	"

Panchayat Samithis

In the ordinary Samithi of the sample, all the woman representatives were coopted members. Not even a single woman became the member of the Samithi in the capacity of Sarpanch. The position in the advanced Samithi was better and encouraging than that in the ordinary Samithi. This Samithi consisted of coopted as well as ex-officio women members (who became members in the capacity of Sarpanches). This is clear from Table 5.2.

TABLE 5.2
Women Representatives of Advanced Samithi

Period	Required No. of woman representatives	Actual No. of woman representatives	No. of coopted woman representatives	No. of woman Sarpanches
1959-64	2	3	3	Nil
1964-70	4	6	5	1
1970-76	4	7	6	1
1981-87	2	2	2	Nil

Note: During 1976-81 the Panchayat Samithis functioned under special officers.

The table reveals a significant increase in the number of coopted members during 1964-70 and ex-officio members during 1970-76. The rise in the figure of coopted members during 1964-70 was due to the resignation of some members and the cooption of substitute members. The increase in the ex-officio membership during 1970-76 was on account of the policy adopted by Congress (N) to provide increased representation of women in the legislative bodies.

Zilla Parishad

The position of women representatives in the Zilla Parishad is given in Table 5.3.

TABLE 5.3
Women Members of the Zilla Parishad

Period	Ex-officio women members	Ordinary women members	Coopted women members	Total
1959-64	2	Nil	2	4
1964-70	-	1	6	7
1970-76	5	1	4	10
1978-81	1	-	-	1
1981-87	2	-	2	4
1987-	5	-	-	5

Note: The Zilla Parishads in the State from 1976-81 functioned under special officers. However, the MLAs and Ministers used to be associated with the administration of the districts. Since 1987, the principle of cooption is given up.

Socio-Economic and Political Background

The socio-economic background in general and political background in particular are important determinants of shaping the nature and level of participation of members in political institutions. Education, economic position, age, caste, awareness, political background and experience in bodies other than political associations are taken as indicators to study the socio-economic and political background in the present context.

I. Education

The respondents in the sample are divided into four groups — illiterates, members with elementary educational qualification, members with secondary educational qualification and members with higher educational qualification. The educational background of the women members of the Gram Panchayats, Panchayat Samithis and the Zilla Parishads under study can be noted from Tables 5.4, 5.5 and 5.6

TABLE 5.4
Women Members of Gram Panchayats: Levels of Education

	Gram Panchayat of the Ordinary Samithi				*Gram Panchayat of the Advanced Samithi*			
	Gram Panchayat of the Backward village		Gram Panchayat of the Advanced village		Gram Panchayat of the Advanced village		Gram Panchayat of the Backward village	
	No. of women	%	No. of women	%	No. of women	%	No. of women	%
Illiterates	5	83.33	3	33.33	2	33.33	3	33.33
Elementary Education	1	16.67	3	33.33	4	66.67	4	44.44
Secondary Education	Nil	Nil	3	33.33	Nil	Nil	2	22.22
Higher Education	Nil	Nil	Nil	Nil	Nil	Nil	Nil	Nil

Note: Of the 30 women members of the Gram Panchayats in the sample 43.33% were found to be illiterates, 40% had elementary educational qualification and 16.66% received higher education.

TABLE 5.5
Educational Levels of the Women Members in Samithis

	Ordinary Samithi		Advanced Samithi	
	No. of women	%	No. of women	%
Illiterates	3	17.64	1	6.66
Elementary Education	13	76.48	8	53.34
Secondary Education	1	5.88	6	40.00
Higher Education	Nil	Nil	Nil	Nil

TABLE 5.6
Educational Levels of Zilla Parishad Women Members

	No. of women	Percentage
Illiterates	Nil	Nil
Elementary Education	3	15.80
Secondary Education	8	42.10
Higher Education	8	42.10

The Table reveals that illiterate members were less in the Samithis when compared to Gram Panchayats. In both the Samithis put together, women with elementary educational qualification formed a majority (65.63%).

Zilla Parishad

In the Zilla Parishad, women with secondary and higher educational qualifications form a majority. This is clear from Table 5.6.

II. Economic Status

TABLE 5.7
Economic Position of Women Members of Gram Panchayats

Categories	*Gram Panchayats of the Ordinary Samithi*				*Gram Panchayats of the Advanced Samithi*			
	Gram Panchayat of the Backward village		Gram Panchayat of the Advanced village		Gram Panchayat of the Backward village		Gram Panchayat of the Advanced village	
	No.	%	No.	%	No.	%	No.	%
Poor	6	100.00	2	22.22	3	50.00	2	22.22
Middle Class	Nil	Nil	5	55.55	3	50.00	6	66.66
Rich	Nil	Nil	1	22.22			1	11.11

Note: It is evident from the Table that poor and middle class women form a majority in the Gram Panchayats.

Panchayat Samithis

In the Panchayat Samithis a majority of women belonged to middle class families which is clear from Table 5.8.

TABLE 5.8
Economic Status of the Women Members of Panchayat Samithis

Categories	Ordinary Samithi		Advanced Samithi	
	No. of women	%	No. of women	%
Poor	2	11.80	1	6.66
Middle Class	11	64.70	13	86.68
Rich	4	23.50	1	6.66

It should be noted here that the percentage of women representatives of rich classes is more in the ordinary Samithi than that in the advanced Samithi. The reason is that in the ordinary Samithi, during 1970-76, all the coopted women members to the

Samithi were either relatives or friends of the President of the Samithi who was a very rich man. His relatives and friends were also rich.

Zilla Parishad

In the Zilla Parishad, the rich classes formed a majority as will be clear from Table 5.9.

TABLE 5.9
Economic Status of the Women Members of Zilla Parishad

Categories	No of Women	Percentage
Poor	Nil	Nil
Middle class	8	42.10
Rich	11	57.89

A general survey of the economic position of the women members in the sample reveals that in the Gram Panchayats, the poor and middle class women find greater representation, in the Panchayat Samithis, a majority of women belong to middle class and in the Zilla Parishad/ Zilla Praja Parishad, rich women are in majority.

III. Age

Age is a very important factor influencing the degree of participation. In general, young and middle aged could be expected to participate actively in any institution. For the purposes of determining the age groups of the members in the sample, those whose age falls between 18 and 35 are treated as young. Women whose age falls between 36 to 50 years are regarded as middle aged and those whose age is above 50 are treated as old. The age-wise analysis of the members of the Gram Panchayats, Panchayat Samithis and Zilla Parishad/Zilla Praja Parishads under study can be seen from Table 5.10.

The Table reveals that young women form a majority in the Ordinary Samithi and in the Advanced Samithi, a majority women members were middle aged.

In the Zilla Parishad, of the 19 members interviewed, nine (47.37%) are young, seven (36.84%) are middle aged and three (15.79%) are old.

TABLE 5.10
Age-wise Distribution of Women Members of Gram Panchayats

	Gram Panchayats of Ordinary Samithi				*Gram Panchayats of Advanced Samithi*			
	Gram Panchayat of Backward village		Gram Panchayat of Advanced village		Gram Panchayat of Backward village		Gram Panchayat of Advanced village	
	No.	%	No.	%	No.	%	No.	%
Young	1	16.66	Nil	Nil	3	50.00	5	55.55
Middle Aged	Nil	Nil	7	77.78	1	16.66	3	33.33
Old	5	83.33	2	22.22	2	33.33	1	11.11

Note: The Table makes clear that in the Gram Panchayats of the backward villages, old aged women are preferred to the young and middle aged.

TABLE 5.11
Age-wise Distribution of Women Members of Samithis

Age Group	Ordinary Samithi		Advanced Samithi	
	No.	%	No.	%
Young	9	52.94	5	33.34
Middle Aged	5	29.42	10	66.66
Old	3	17.64	Nil	Nil

IV. Caste

Caste plays a very significant role in Indian politics and has greater significance in village politics. The caste-wise distribution of women members can be noted in Tables 5.12, 5.13, 5.14 and 5.15.

TABLE 5.12
Caste-wise Distribution of Women Members of Gram Panchayats of Backward Villages

Caste	Gram Panchayat of Backward village of the Ordinary Samithi			Gram Panchayat of Backward village of the Advanced Samithi	
	No.	%	Caste	No.	%
Backward classes	5	83.33	Backward Classes	4	66.66
Scheduled Castes	1	16.66	Scheduled Castes	1	16.66
Scheduled Tribes	Nil	Nil	Scheduled Tribes	1	16.66

TABLE 5.13
Caste-wise Distribution of Women Members of Gram Panchayats of Advanced Villages

Caste	Gram Panchayat of the Advanced Village of Ordinary Samithi		Caste	Gram Panchayat of the Advanced Village of Advanced Samithi	
	No.	%		No.	%
Backward Classes	5	55.55	Kapu	3	33.33
Scheduled Castes	1	11.11	Brahmin	2	22.22
Christians	1	11.11	Vysya	1	11.11
Vysya S	1	11.11	Backward Classes	3	33.33
Agnikula Kshatriya S	1	11.11			

Panchayat Samithis

The Panchayat Samithis in the sample consist of women belonging to different castes. In these bodies women from backward classes form a single majority group which becomes evident from the Table 5.14.

Zilla Parishad

In the Zilla Parishad as in the case of Panchayat Samithis, the women members from the Kapu caste formed a single majority group.

TABLE 5.14
Caste-wise Distribution of the Women Members of Panchayat Samithis

Caste	Ordinary Samithi		Caste	Advanced Samithi	
	No.	%		No.	%
Kapu	8	47.06	Kapu	5	33.33
Kamma	2	11.76	Vysya	1	6.67
Kalavantas	2	11.76	Brahmins	2	13.33
Backward class	1	5.88	Backward classes	6	40.00
Chitrikaranam	1	5.88			
Brahmins	1	5.88	Scheduled castes	1	6.67
Scheduled Castes	1	5.88			

TABLE 5.15
Caste-wise Distribution of Women Members of Zilla Parishad

Caste	Number of Women	Percentage
Kapu	6	31.60
Brahmins	3	15.78
Kshtriya	2	10.52
Vysya	1	5.26
Kamma	1	5.26
Scheduled Castes	3	15.78
Backward Class	3	15.78

V. Awareness

The awareness of the respondents is tested on the basis of a set of questions forming part of the questionnaire. The awareness of those who do not have any knowledge of the purposes and functions of the institutions in which they served is treated as 'Nil'. The awareness of the members who know the composition and functions of these institutions is regarded as "Average". Those members who showed clear knowledge of these aspects, functions of the executive officers and functions of the standing committee especially the committee dealing with woman welfare and child welfare is considered 'Fair'. In the Gram Panchayats, 70% of the women members have 'Nil' awareness, 16.67% have showed 'Average' awareness and 13.33% are found to be possessing 'Fair' awareness. One must note that the degree of awareness has shown an increasing trend. The writer has come across some women members who know and care for needs of their villages. Some women who got elected in 1981 have rendered considerable service to their villages. Many have shown anxiety to enlighten themselves about the purposes and functions of Panchayati Raj institutions. This anxiety is more visible in the advanced villages than in the backward villages.

Panchayat Samithis

The awareness of the women members of the Samithis in the sample can be seen from Table 5. 16.

TABLE 5.16
Awareness of Women Members of Panchayat Samithis

Ordinary Samithi			Advanced Samithi		
Degree of Awareness	No.	Percentage	Degree of Awareness	No.	Percentage
Nil	14	82.35	Nil	9	60.00
Average	3	17.65	Average	6	40.00
Fair	Nil	Nil	Fair	Nil	Nil

The Table reveals that the advanced Samithi is in a better position than the ordinary Samithi.

Zilla Parishad

In the Zilla Parishad four members (21.05%) have 'nil' awareness 11 members (57.89%) have 'average' awareness and four (21.05%) have 'fair' awareness. The greater degree of awareness in the Zilla Parishad members, to a large extent, is due to the impact of modernisation and urbanisation and relatively higher educational levels.

VI. Political Background

The women members of the Gram Panchayats under study do not have any previous experience in politics at the time of their election to these bodies. In the backward villages a woman or women, as the case may be, used to be elected for consecutive terms. But this practice did not enable them to gain experience. However, it is important to note that in the elections of 1987, in both the backward villages, new women members have been chosen.

Panchayat Samithis

In the ordinary Samithi no woman had political experience before her entry into the Samithi. But in the advanced Samithi, only three women constituting about 20% had experience in politics. Of these three, the experience of two was concerned with canvassing in elections and one woman served as member of a Gram Panchayat.

Zilla Parishad

In the Zilla Parishad, a majority of woman, i.e. 10 (52.63%) have experience in politics. Participation in the freedom struggle, convassing in elections and serving as MLAs, municipal councillors and sarpanches are the activities in general in which woman members with political experience took part. Those who participated in the freedom struggle underwent imprisonment also.

Membership in Bodies other than Political Institutions

Membership in different associations and institutions enables the participants to become active, develop comprehensive and realistic understanding of the problems under consideration and acquire status. The position in the sample in this aspect is the following:

In three Gram Panchayats (two Gram Panchayats of the two backward villages and the Gram Panchayat of advanced village in the sample) women members had no association with anybody other than the Gram Panchayats. But in the advanced village of the advanced Samithi, two women have membership in Mahila Mandals. Of these two, one member was for some time the President of a Mahila Mandal.

Panchayat Samithis

In the ordinary Samithi, eight members (47.06%) had no association at all, seven (41.18%) have nominal association and two (11.70%) had active association with other associations. Membership in other associations is mostly nominal in the ordinary Samithi. The situation is not also encouraging in the advanced Samithi. On this Samithi 10 women (66.67%) were not members of any other association, two (13.33%) had nominal association with Mahila Mandals and the remaining three (20%) were active members of Mahila Mandals. Of these three, one woman served as one of the Directors of a Mahila Super Bazar.

Zilla Parishad

The position of the women members of the Zilla Parishad was better in respect of membership in other association. 11 members of the Zilla Parishad (57.89%) had membership in other associations and the rest, i.e. eight (42.10%) did not have. In most cases, the membership was active and not nominal. A few examples can be given here. Smt. Y. Savitri Devi, who served on the Zilla Parishad in the capacity of a coopted as well as an ex-officio member had and now has membership in various associations like Mahila Cooperative Stores, Ladies Recreation Club, Guild of Services, Red Cross Society and several other social and cultural organisations. To give another example, Smt. G. Kamaladevi, who is more interested in social service than in politics served as the Vice-President and Secretary of the Ladies' Recreation Club of her place, Vice-President and Joint-Secretary of Guild of Services, First Class Bench Magistrate, Secretary, Women's Educational Society, Vice-President, Mahila Super Bazar, Secretary, Hindi Premimandali and Joint-Secretary of the Committee constituted for the construction of Kalayana Mandapam in Kakinada. Another example is that of a Mahila Mandal President, K. Prabhavati. Under her presidentship, the Mahila Mandal of her village became an ideal association within a very short period of its establishment.

The above analysis should not lead one to conclude that all the active members of social associations would effectively participate in the political institutions also. Purely personal interests and status consciousness come in the way of effective participation. Sometimes, the presence of status conscious and arrogant women hinders rather than prove helpful in taking decisions easily and effectively.

Women Members of Mandala Praja Parishads

The writer has come across six women members of Mandala Praja Parishads of which five are women presidents and the remaining a coopted member from religious minorities. The coopted member, aged 20, has secondary educational qualification and entered her position for the first time. She belongs to a middle class family. Hers is only a Sarpanch supporting role in the Mandal to which she is coopted.

Of 5 presidents in the sample, one has higher educational qualification and all the others have secondary educational qualifications. Four of five presidents came from rich families and the one came from a middle class family. Two of them are young and three middle aged. Two of the presidents belong to forward castes and three to backward classes. Their entry into politics started with their contesting elections. In the case of all the presidents, the contests have been direct and tough. Two of the five presidents have 'fair' awareness and the other three 'average' awareness.

Members of All Women Panchayat

The need for a study of the socio-economic and political background of the members of all women-panchayat, in relation to participation does not arise at all because the panchayat never functioned with women members participation in it.

Impact of Socio-Economic and Political Background On Participation

The study revealed that:

(1) Education and participation are interrelated. In general, women members having secondary educational qualification and more participated well in the meetings.

(2) The economic position is another important factor that determines the extent of participation. Economic status given a sense of confidence and encouragement to participate. The participation of the poor women members is found mostly insignificant. The middle class and rich members showed greater degree of participation.

(3) Age has its impact on participation. The extent of participation of the young and middle aged is generally more than that of the old aged.

(4) Caste has greater relevance in the selection of members than in participation.

(5) Awareness and participation are closely related. The extent of

participation is determined by the level of awareness.

(6) Women members with experience in politics played active roles in the institutions under study.

(7) Membership in bodies other than political associations did not contribute to greater level of participation in political institutions. On the other hand, most of the women members in the sample who are also members of other associations are more interested in social service than in politics.

(8) Last, but not least, point of importance is that personal interest and active participation are very closely related.

6
Women Presiding Officers

THE position one holds in an institution is one of the very important factors that determines the effectiveness of the role of the person. Members in key positions will have greater opportunities of playing prominent roles when compared to other members. The presiding officers hold key positions and hence could play significant roles by directing and controlling the whole process of decision-making.

The writer has come across 12 presiding officers. A study of their roles as popular heads of the representative institutions would throw light on their status as members in key positions. Of these 12, one is the President of a Samithi, five are Sarpanches of villages, one is the Upa Sarpanch of a village, and the other five are the Presidents of the Mandala Praja Parishads which came into existence in 1987. As pointed out earlier, 9% of the offices of presiding officers of Mandala Praja Parishads are reserved for women and all the five women presiding officers in the sample are those that won the presidentships that are reserved for women. The factors leading to the selection of these women to their positions, their participation, achievements and other related matters are studied in this chapter.

Women Sarpanches

The women Sarpanches in the sample could be divided into two categories — (1) Nominal Sarpanches and (2) Real Sarpanches. The Nominal Sarpanches are those that are put in their positions as a mere formality and their functions are exercised by some others. The Real Sarpanches are those that practically exercised these functions. Of the 5 Sarpanches in the sample, four are nominal and only a single Sarpanch is real. The details of the roles of these two categories of Sarpanches are given below:

(1) *Nominal Sarpanches:* In the case of two of the four nominal Sarpanches the bar or the restriction that government officials are not

entitled to be elected as popular representatives is the reason that led to their selection as Sarpanches. This point is frankly admitted by the husbands of these Sarpanches at the time of interview. It is important to note that it is only the husbands and not the women Sarpanches that responded to the writer's questions at the time of interview. The husbands of these Sarpanches were the Village Munsifs. They could not contest because of official position, but wanted to assume political positions. Hence they managed that their wives got elected as Sarpanches and consequently combined in themselves, conveniently, political as well as official roles. One of the two women Sarpanches mentioned above merely used to sign in the registers after the meetings are conducted and decisions are taken by the Gram Panchayats with the husband in the chair.

One of the four nominal Sarpanches in the sample has been co-opted to the Zilla Parishad during 1970-76 and had also served as the member of the Gannavaram Panchayat Samithi in the capacity of Sarpanch. She had also been the president of the Mahila Mandal of her village. Her role in all these institutions was insignificant and it was her husband that functioned as the Sarpanch in reality. The husband used to accompany the woman Sarpanch to all the meetings of the Panchayat Samithi and the Zilla Parishad. Certain developmental activities like construction of roads, providing water supply and building schools had taken place in the village during her formal incumbency.

The third nominal woman Sarpanch was the Sarpanch of a Gram Panchayat where the office of Sarpanch is reserved for the Scheduled Tribes under the state system of reservation. The fact is that, the village has only a handful of Scheduled Tribes. The appearance of a larger number of Scheduled Tribes voters in the electoral roles took place under certain peculiar circumstances. During the time of enlisting voters in the area, several Scheduled Tribes people came to the village as casual immigrant labourers. They were all entered into the electoral rolls and this provided the basis for reserving the Sarpanchship to a Scheduled Tribe candidate. In reality under the circumstances stated above, the hitherto Sarpanch of the village (He belonged to Settibalija community, a backward caste) managed to see that an illiterate Scheduled Tribe woman is unanimously elected as the Sarpanch of Turpulanka village in the Amalapuram Panchayat Samithi of the East Godavari District of Andhra Pradesh. Of course, the practice of unanimous election is prevalent in the village ever since the formation of the Gram Panchayat till today. Thus the former Sarpanch of the village who became the Upa Sarpanch became the *de-facto* Sarpanch. The case of this woman Sarpanch is a typical example of exploitation of innocent women by the influential members of the villages. The woman Sarpanch said, at the time of interview, that she is made the Sarpanch by the former Sarpanch and in fact she also treats and calls the Upa Sarpanch as the Sarpanch. Her assumption of Sarpanchship led to strained relation with her only daughter because her son-in-law aspired for the office but could not get it due to the intervention of the former Sarpanch. This case is also a clear example of situation-manipulation by local politicians in their anxiety to retain power in their own hands. This state of affairs would retard the growth of democratic leadership. The innocent woman Sarpanch knew the needs of the villagers and had been really interested in the development of the village. Of course, she thought that it should be done by the so-called 'Sarpanch *de-facto*'.

Another nominal Sarpanch came to power in a situation of pique, pride and prejudice on the part of the residents of a village and definitely not out of respect for women and recognition of equality. Another important point is that this woman Sarpanch was heading an all-women Gram Panchayat. It would now be worthwhile to mention the relevant details. The Sarpanchship of the Gram Panchayat of a village in the Warangal District of Andhra Pradesh was reserved for the Scheduled Tribes before the 1981 elections. The village leadership, dominated by a forward community (Kamma caste), tried for the exclusion of this Panchayat from the list of reserved Panchayats. It was actually the opposition among the villagers against having a tribal man as their leader that led to frustration and Gandhinagaram Panchayat becoming an all-women panchayat. The village leaders, when interviewed, said that they could not reconcile themselves to the prospect of a person from a Scheduled Tribe becoming their chief. At the same time, they were aware that the village would get a cash award of five thousand rupees from the State Government if the election was unanimous. They had finally decided that a woman would become the Sarpanch. But the male villagers were unwilling to accept membership in the Gram Panchayat where a woman served as the presiding officer. Thus it turned out that the other members of the Panchayat were also women. Elected under such circumstances, the woman Sarpanch could not be expected to function as an active presiding officer. In fact, the Gram Panchayat did not function from 1981-87 even once with the woman Sarpanch really presiding over the meeting.

(2) *Real Sarpanch:* The real Sarpanch in the sample, Smt. Sitamahalakshmi, as mentioned earlier, was a very active and promising lady. Her Sarpanchship provided a source of inspiration to women. She belonged to middle class, had elementary educational qualifications and was young during her tenure of office. The politics

within a dominating community in the Mukkamala village of the East Godavari District of Andhra Pradesh led to her election as the member of the Gram Panchayat and later as Sarpanch. She was originally disinterested in politics. But having assumed the office, she put forth her maximum effort for the development of the village. The unreserved and complete support of her husband added strength to her interest and activities.

The period of office of this woman Sarpanch could be studied under three phases: (a) the phase of achievements (b) the phase of opposition and challenge and (c) the phase of surrender of Sarpanchship

(a) *The phase of achievements:*

In the early period of her office, the woman Sarpanch had several activities to her credit. Welfare measures like laying 14 roads, improving schools, providing water facility and acquisition of furniture to the Gram Panchayat had been carried out. She was instrumental in getting two sewing-centers established in her village. She could secure the order for the construction of the Gram Panchayat building which was completed later. She was particularly interested in women welfare activities and served as the President of the Mahila Mandal during the period of her Sarpanchship. It is significant that the village is even now regarded as one of the best villages of the Samithi of which it formed part. This recognition is partly due to her initiative and partly due to the well established political culture in the village. The village was one of the centers of political activity during the freedom struggle days. A prominent freedom fighter, Sri Kala Vankata Rao, was brought up there. He also took a significant role in the struggle for the separation of the Telugu speaking areas from the former Madras State in the formation of Andhra State in 1953 and in the establishment of the larger state of Andhra Pradesh in 1956. He himself served as the Revenue Minister of Andhra Pradesh in the early years of its formation.

It must be mentioned here that in places where local political culture has already been established by prominent leaders, the process of political socialisation would become easy and quick. This in turn will produce conditions conducive to development.

(b) *The phase of opposition and challenge:*

As one study made it clear, the Panchayati Raj system is a double-edged weapon and is capable of working at cross purposes.[1] This fact could be seen in the case under study. In this case, a sudden switch over of some members of the Gram Panchayat to the opposition group created several hurdles to the woman Sarpanch. As it generally happens, the opposition group has been led by an aspirant to the Sarpanchship, who could not get it due to local factional politics. Whatever welfare measures the woman Sarpanch proposed used to be voted down by the opposing majority newly formed. Due to the opposition she could not even buy a radio set for the Gram Panchayat[2], pay even very meagre amounts, in the form of daily allowance to the clerk,[3] get approved the budget,[4] prepare estimates to provide drainage facilities,[5] and provide bonus to the clerk for his efforts in the speedy collection of revenues.[6] The opposition was so intense and acute that the position of the woman Sarpanch became extremely inconvenient.

(c) *The phase of surrender of Sarpanchship:*

The woman Sarpanch, as has been mentioned above, has to face constant challenge and opposition which in turn led to deadlocks. The government then has taken a decision to appoint a special officer to take over the administration of the village. In spite of her enthusiasm and devoted work, the woman Sarpanch had to surrender her office.

In this connection it is essential to discuss how dead-locks relating to passing of resolutions proposed by a Sarpanch in a Gram Panchayat arise and how they are overcome. Such deadlocks come in when a Sarpanch could not win the confidence of a majority of members of the Gram Panchayat. This may happen either because of the irresponsible behaviour of the Sarpanch or due to factional politics. It should also be mentioned that in the case of woman Sarpanches, it is the inability of the Gram Panchayat members to accept the leadership of a woman, particularly an assertive woman, that leads to tensions and strong opposition to the Sarpanch of a new Gram Panchayat. One way of resolving or avoiding deadlocks is to remove the Sarpanch from office by a vote of no-confidence by the Gram Panchayat itself and to elect a new Sarpanch. The other way is that of suspending the Gram Panchayat and forming a new Gram Panchayat. Of the above two means the first is more convenient to the Gram Panchayat, because matters could be settled without inviting government intervention. In the villages where intense factionalism exists, there is the likelihood of deliberate engineering of dead-locks only with a view to getting the suspension of the Gram Panchayat and to invite the intervention of government. Such an atmosphere is not conducive to the development of villages.

The Real Sarpanch as an Ex-officio Member of the Samithi

Coming back to the role of the lady Sarpanch, in other respects, too, participation of the real Sarpanch in the Panchayat Samithi is remarkable. She proved herself very courageous and assertive in expressing her views. She could persuade and convince the Panchayat Samithi members, as well as officers, and get necessary grants for improvement measures. Her participation was so inspiring that she could win over her opponents to her side. She had firm conviction that the popular representatives should work only for public and not private interests. An example can be cited here. Once the lady proposed in the Samithi that a particular person be appointed to a certain post, the President of the Samithi replied that they would have considered her request favourably if the person recommended is her relative or friend. The woman Sarpanch immediately reacted to the Samithi President's reply and fearlessly said that the Samithi members are not there to promote the selfish interests of friends and relatives and that they should always keep public interest in their mind.

Problems of the Real Sarpanch

The Real Sarpanch had to face peculiar problems mentioned below:

(i) She came from an upper caste orthodox family. Even in the 60s, acceptance of membership in the political institutions by the upper caste orthodox family ladies was highly objectionable from the social milieu angle. Her election to the Gram Panchayat very greatly offended her father, who said that he was ashamed that she was born to him. But the present trend is that women's membership in these institutions is accepted, though active participation is not encouraged.

(ii) She had to face indirect threats from her relations that she would be declared an out-caste. There had been threats to her life as well as her husband's and children's lives. At the time of interview, the husband of the woman Sarpanch told that he used to sleep outside the house so that anyone who comes to kill them would kill him first and then his wife and children.

(iii) She had to face the problem of not receiving notices of Panchayat Samithi's meeting sufficiently in advance. She felt that there had been deliberate attempts to keep her away from the meetings.

(iv) Lack of awareness of the rules was another factor that proved a source of inconvenience to this Sarpanch. Both the Sarpanch and her husband said "we did not know the rule position. Hence we had to go to other places to know the implications of the rules"

On the one hand, there appears in the woman Sarpanch a very great satisfaction for her achievements and on the other, a feeling of distress for having faced several problems. She has since left the political career and the village also, and is now engaged in household duties and religious observances.

Upa Sarpanch (Vice-President)

The writer has come across an Upa Sarpanch elected in the year 1987 in Mukkamala village, in the East Godavari District of Andhra Pradesh. She is young, educated belonging to a Backward Caste and , given the chance, can prove to be an active participant. According to the Andhra Pradesh Gram Panchayat Act, the Upa Sarpanch (Vice-President) of a Gram Panchayat is to be elected by the members of the Gram Panchayat. In fact, election to this office in this village did not take place and she got unanimously elected as the Upa Sarpanch on the suggestion of the Sarpanch. When the writer interviewed the Sarpanch of the village, he said that he made her the Vice-President, because she is an intelligent and educated girl and also because he wanted to make a woman, the Upa Sarpanch. Another important factor that contributed to her selection is that the Vice-Presidentship has been given to a Scheduled Caste member until then and in the year 1987 it was decided that it should go to a Backward Caste member. The present woman Upa Sarpanch in this case belongs to this community and this as well as the strong support of her father, who served as a member of the Gram Panchayat of the same village for 25 years, led to her selection to this key position.

The 20-year old lady member when interviewed has been found enthusiastic and having a fair degree of awareness of the needs of the villagers. But her participation (the participation of other members of the Gram Panchayat also) gets heavily, perhaps totally, restricted because the decisions are taken by the Sarpanch himself and implemented. Of course, a majority of the villagers and the members in the Gram Panchayat feel that the Sarpanch has been helpful to them in developing the village. Thus the village came to be ruled by a single benevolent Sarpanch.

Women Samithi President

The Sample consists of a woman who served as the President of the Kapileswarapuram Panchayat Samithi in the district. The woman president, Mrs. Balusu Rajarajeswaramma, belongs to a very rich family, had secondary educational qualification and has a very good political background. Her father-in-law was the proprietor of the Kapileswarapuram estate in the Peddapuram Samasthanam of British India. Some of her relations are even members of the Indian Parliament. Her husband was himself the Chairman of the East Godavari Zilla Parishad. He is an industrialist, a member of the

Andhra Pradesh Legislative Council, Andhra University Senate and headed several important and influential associations. In short, she has all the conditions necessary to emerge as a very successful Panchayat Samithi President.

The woman President entered politics at the age of 37 as a coopted member of the Kapileswarapuram Panchayat Samithi in 1964 and became the President only a few days after cooption as member. The election of her husband who was till then the President of the Samithi as the Zilla Parishad Chairman in 1964 led to her election as the President. Thus the attempts to see that the office of president does not go out of the family is the chief reason for this woman getting elected. Of course, this did not imply that the woman president was not talented, interested, deserving or active. The support of her wealthy husband and other family members who have important political positions added strength to her successful functioning.

Achievements

Under the presidentship of Mrs. Balusu Rajarajeswaramma, the Samithi was credited with remarkable progress. As a detailed account is not possible, a few examples can be given to show the nature of progress and achievements in the Samithi.

There was notable development in the fields of agriculture, fishing, animal husbandry, family planning, uplift of backward classes, health and education. In the year 1968-69, the Samithi started the three crop plan on an experimental measure and was successful in implementing it on a permanent basis. On more than one occasion, the Samithi received prizes for highest rice-production in the district. During 1969-70, the Samithi received an award for conducting the maximum number of family planning operations in the district. In 1968-69 the Samithi was adjudged as the best Samithi in mobilising small-savings by women.

During the Presidentship of Mrs. Balusu Rajarajeswaramma, several woman welfare measures like the establishment of Mahila Mandals, conducting competitions for women and establishing sewing, embroidery, knitting and weaving centres have been undertaken. A special point worthy of mention is that the president of a village Mahila Mandal in the Samithi (Gangararam village) was elected as the President of the district level Mahila Mandali in the early 80s. The village earned reputation as having nursed a very efficient Mahila Mandal under her leadership. The woman president herself said that "woman used to come forward because a woman is the president of the Samithi."

When asked about the problems of a woman President, she replied that "problems are everywhere. We must push aside the problems and clear our path." The President feels that it is the co-operation of the Sarpanches and officers that led to her success.

The woman welfare measures during this period should not lead one to conclude that the woman president has taken every care to see that the funds allotted to woman welfare are fully utilised. The records of the Samithi show that every year there were large unspent balances (ranging from Rs. 9,000 to 33,000) of the funds earmarked for women welfare.

Thus woman president gave up political life and is presently staying in a city, where she is the life member of Ladies Recreation Club, Andhra Mahila Sabha and Horticultural Association in Madras.

Presidents of Mandala Praja Parishads

As stated earlier, the Andhra Pradesh Mandala Praja Parishads, Zilla Praja Parishads and Zilla Pranalika Abhivrudhi Sameeksha Mandals Act, 1986 brought about significant changes in respect of women's representation in key positions. It ensured 9% of the presiding officers' positions to women. This had led to the reservation and election of 2 Zilla Parishad Presidentships and 96 Mandala Praja Parishad Presidentships for women in Andhra Pradesh. Apart from these, for three unreserved Mandala Praja Parishads, one Mandala Praja Parishad reserved for SC and one Mandala Praja Parishad reserved for BC, women became the presiding officers. Therefore, in the state of Andhra Pradesh, there are, at present, 2 Zilla Praja Parishad Presidents and 101 Women Mandala Praja Parishad Presidents. These figures would indicate that a quantitative betterment in respect of women's position in leadership roles is possible by means of reservation and proper selections would definitely lead to qualitative improvement too.

The writer has interviewed some Presidents of Mandala Praja Parishads in the month of June 1989, and the circumstances leading to the assumption of the prestigious positions by some women need detailed examination. Of course, these cases would not facilitate making generalisations, but would clearly indicate the emergence of a new young woman leadership. The situation would reveal a revitalisation trend in the functioning of Panchayat Raj.

The writer has come across some active and effective woman presidents during her very recent study. For instance, Mallela Gowri, the president of Bikkavole Mandala Praja Parishad in Andhra Pradesh is very much aware of the organisation and functions of the institution she heads. At the time of interview, she said that she could contest and become the president because of the fact that the position is reserved for women and in the absence of this, her father-in-law who served as the Sarpanch of the Bikkavole Gram Panchayat for over 25 years would have contested for the Mandala Praja Parishad.

In the two years of her presidentship under the Village Development Scheme, with an expenditure of 14 lakhs and 20 thousand, eight roads have been laid, some school buildings have been constructed at a cost of Rs. 2,25,000 and self-employment opportunities for landless poor are provided for and protected water schemes taken up. Subsidised loans for 305 persons, in addition to loans for 207 Scheduled Caste persons, have been distributed. In addition to these, works which include financial assistance for water facilities to fields, construction of biogas plants, supply of plants to ryots, small scale grant of loans for the rearing of cows, purchase of furniture to schools, provision of scholarships for Scheduled Caste students, supply of textbooks to poor students and distribution of clothes for Scheduled Tribe students have been undertaken.[7]

It is very important to point out that in the male dominated Mandal Praja Parishad, the only woman, who is also its President finds no problem in conducting the proceedings and arriving at consensus. The contributing factors have been her higher education, general awareness level, political background, cooperation of the officials, her urban-living till her marriage and, above all, her ability and interest.

Another active woman President is Smt. Parvathi, a young and energetic lady, who occupied this position on her own initiative. When she came to know of the reservation of Anaparthi Mandal Presidentship to a woman she informed her desire initially to her husband, who at the first instance reacted negatively and tauntingly posed her the question "will you occupy a stage and speak?" But Parvathi could convince her husband that her taking political career would not come in the way of her domestic functions and thus could successfully convert him to her idea of contesting. Her wishes in this regard received support from local political leaders. All these positive trends facilitated her success.

During the 2 years of her Presidentship, 149 individuals have been benefited under the housing facilities schemes meant for weaker sections and 404 would receive benefits during 1988-89. A number of individuals have been given the benefit of *Chettu Patta Scheme* (a scheme according to which plants like cocoanut plants, would be supplied free of cost to poor and they would be allowed to grow them on government lands). This is a measure intended to provide a sort of self-occupation to the poor. Other measures taken during this period include construction of school buildings and staff quarters, digging of borewells, providing medical facilities, adopting maternity and childwelfare measures, protecting animals, providing irrigation facilities and providing audio-visual facilities to schools and community centres.[8]

A remarkable achievement during 1988-89 in the Anaparthi Mandal is that cent per cent taxes have been collected. In the very first year of the woman President's tenure, Anaparthi Gram Panchayat has been adjudged as the best Gram Panchayat in the Mandal. While the credit for this partly goes to the former president, this achievement would definitely be a source of inspiration to the present woman-president, who lives in Anaparthi village proper.

Smt. Parvathi visits all the Gram Panchayats in the Mandal once in a month and personally supervises the works in progress. Her abilities for ensuring effective performance of development works are also noteworthy. She is in the habit of personally instructing her aides as to how works should be implemented. If she found that her instructions have not been paid heed to, she did not hesitate in giving a warning and finally a memo, in case the warning proved unfruitful. This style of functioning brought her many benefits.

One of the important problems faced by this woman president is the absence of adequate cooperation by the Mandal Officers, like Mandal Revenue Officer and the Mandal Development Officer. This attitude is reported to be due to the connections that they have to a party opposed to the party to which the president belongs. The woman Sarpanch said that in addition to this, the bureaucrats have a tendency to defend themselves as a group against the popular representatives and this would lead to inaction on the part of superior officers. They would be reluctant to setting things right even after complaints have been made to them against some lower officials. There have been occasions when the superior officials openly supported their brethren in the presence of public representatives without making even preliminary inquiries. A tendency of this type in the officials would develop an attitude of carelessness towards the political leaders and this, in its turn, would hamper the implementation of development projects.

Another problem facing her and which is acknowledged by this woman Sarpanch is her ignorance of English language. She has studied up to 9th class and says that when she receives letters or representations in English, she has to wait till the return of her husband home. To avoid this difficulty and to herself learn English, she engaged a tutor. But she says that her domestic responsibilities would not give her sufficient leisure to learn English in a short time. Still, the woman Sarpanch is found very determined to learn English and overcome the difficulty she is facing personally. She says that role-conflict is definitely there but atmosphere of understanding in the family will provide encouragement to women to assume effective leadership roles.

Some other problems of a routine nature like red-tape, corruption have been experienced by the above woman Sarpanch.

In the case of some woman Presidents for Panchayat bodies, the initiative of local MLAs have led to these women contesting for the positions. For instance, in a Congress dominated Mandal in Andhra Pradesh, the Congress MLA persuaded a retired military employee to bring his wife into contest which finally led to her success. This woman Sarpanch and her husband function as a husband-wife team, of course, with the husband taking a very prominent part. In spite of the fact that this woman Sarpanch has not come to the office on her own initiative and interest, has taken her duties and functions in right earnest. She would preside over the meetings of the Mandala Praja Parishad, initiate resolutions and participate in discussion. The case of this woman President is not one of total silence at all as in the case of woman Sarpanches of some Gram Panchayats mentioned earlier. The husband of this woman Sarpanch attends the meetings of the Mandala Praja Parishad and occasionally participates in discussions, but the wife does not function on her own steam, as it were.

There have been women who became presidents on the initiative of their sons. An interesting case in this regard came up during the writer's recent field-work. A young local leader of the Telugu Desam Party in Andhra Pradesh wanted to contest for the presidentship of the Mandala Praja Parishad of his native area but the presidentship of the Mandal has been reserved for woman. Hence, he persuaded his mother to enter the election fray and got her elected. This woman President would formally discharge the functions of the President, would address public meetings and attend to other ceremonial duties also.

Another woman presiding officer came to power on the initiative of her husband. But in this case, it is the husband that takes charge of all the responsibilities of the President. During interviews, the husband, who has been the Sarpanch of his native village till the year of election of his wife as Mandala Praja Parishad President said that his wife contested because the seat is reserved for ladies and admitted that her role is very formal. He alleged that the Telugu Desam Government has earmarked for women those Mandals which are problematic.

The above study of the woman presiding officers reveals that given the opportunity, talented and interested woman could play very effective leadership roles in politics.

References

1. Ram Reddy, G. Social Composition of Panchayati Raj: Background of political Executives in Andhra, *Economic and Political Weekly*, Vol. II p. 2214.

2. Resolution No. 44 dated 30.12.65 and Resolution No. 51 dated 30.3.66 of the Gram Panchayat.
3. Resolution No. 48 dated 28.2.66.
4. Resolution No. 49 dated 2.3.66
5. Resolution No. 10 dated 30.7.66
6. Resolution No. 15 dated 30.7.66.
7. (a) *Andhra Bhoomi* (A Telugu Daily) *Anubandham,* dated 22.5.1989, p. 1, (b) Interview with the president on 3.6.1989.
8. (a) Interview with the president on 3.6.1989, (b) Samskhipta Samacharamu Mariyu Abhivrudhi Karyakramamulapai Nivedika, Mandala Praja Parishad, Anaparthi, dated 25.4.1989 (Report on the Development Activities of the Mandala Praja Parishad, Anaparthi).

7
Conclusion and Recommendations

THE discussion in the preceding chapters would support the argument that in rural India, the generation of 'Stri Shakti' is inadequate and the utilization of even this existing 'Shakti' is not optimum. The realization that adequate partnership of women in the process of development, aimed at the construction of a more equitable, healthy and prosperous societies is important, is still marginal.[1] The fact that when women achieve a share in political power, many things besides politics profoundly change and that political participation is more in the nature of a catalyst bringing about far wider changes in the social system is not sufficiently recognised. With this in the background, it is proposed to discuss the obstacles coming in the way of rural women entering and participating in the political process and to suggest steps for a meaningful participation of rural women in politics particularly in the rural local political bodies.

IMPEDIMENTS

The impediments for women's entry and active participation are too many. For a woman domestic work comes first, work outside the home next and politics is only the third and additional, peripheral role. The constraints or impediments could broadly be divided into structural, functional, attitudinal and environmental. A detailed discussion of these constraints is attempted in the following paragraphs.

Structural Constraints

As pointed out earlier, in many States in India and until recently in some States, women's representation on the Panchayati Raj bodies is ensured by means of cooption. A majority of women members of local bodies are coopted. However, the principle of cooption suffers from one great disadvantage. As the Vyas Committee of Rajasthan appointed to study the Panchayati Raj institutions pointed out, this principle generates a feeling among the elected members that it is only their generosity that gives opportunity to the coopted members to participate in the proceedings.[2] Experience in many States has revealed that the application of cooption method resulted in nominal induction of women members into Panchayati Raj bodies in many cases and that the participation of these members in most cases is minimal. This is not to deny the presence of women members who assumed moderately assertive roles though nominally inducted. But such cases are few. Thus the cooption method proved to be unfruitful due to its inherent weakness.

Functional Constraints

The Panchayati Raj bodies are designed to function as real democratic institutions where the collective will of the rural inhabitants through their representatives should prevail. But in practice, these representative bodies, except in some cases, have become highly centralised. Only those members holding key positions and some influential members and officials dominate the scene. The result is that participation of a majority of the male members as well as the female members has become a formality. This can be illustrated. A male member of the Zilla Parishad in the sample, who served on it in the capacity of MLA said, "in general, the decisions of Zilla Parishad are those of the Chairman and sufficient time is not allotted for discussions. Participation of members in the Zilla Parishad is a failure both for men and women". A woman with good experience in politics said "the decision of the Zilla Parishad and particularly those of the standing committee for women welfare are prior decisions." She further said "to be very frank, there is official domination."

Another important functional constraint is related to the process of recruitment. The recruitment pattern in a large number of Panchayati Raj bodies revealed the absence of careful selection of women members. As pointed out earlier, familial or social nearness to the president (of a panchayat body) have been preferred to knowledge, experience and social service in the choice of women members.

Attitudinal Constraints

Women are made to think and live in a social setting in which politics is regarded as an unsavoury game, dirty profession and so unwomanly. This situation prevents women from assuming active roles in politics even if they enter it. One important point to be mentioned here is that the situation in the 60s was not very different in the so-called developed countries like the United States. In general, orientations and social norms in this country impose restraints on female recruitment, participation and performance. Consequently, women tend to remain in peripheral roles even when they have managed to enter the ranks of the political elite.[3] An important study on American Women in public life has made clear that the husband of a wife in politics may feel that his position as the head of the family is compromised and even that his manhood is challenged.[4] But recent evidence suggests that from 1971 to 1984, the number of women in the State Legislatures in the United States has doubled, that of Congress women increased from 15 to 24, women hold mayoralities in 76 cities as against 7 in 1971 and women have multiplied at the grassroots level in power and voice. In the sub-urban towns and villages, women are found in many numbers as men in chair positions.[5] The State and local levels in America seem to represent the most rapidly changing context for women's representation and participation.[6]

In addition to the above, the feeling that women are meant only for home is more among rural women than the urban women in general. Some examples can be given here. A woman member of the ordinary Samithi in the sample said "we belong to respectable families, we do not go out of our houses. I became a member of the Samithi not because myself and my husband are interested, but only because of the fact that my husband is a very close friend of the president whose request that I should be coopted to the Samithi could not be ignored." It is important to note, as one writer pointed out, governments themselves seem to be endorsing the domesticity of women and the unwaged services they provide for the family.[7]

Many men who wanted their wives to become or who permitted their wives to become members of political institutions are, in fact, against their women taking active roles. There have been many occasions when women members of Gram Panchayats and Panchayat Samithi sat in separate rooms, indicating separate but equal status, while the meetings are being conducted by male members in the scheduled rooms. The argument that man made woman to feel herself as a weaker sex is not unwarranted. However, in the recent years, women are crossing unwanted 'Lakshmanarekhas' which in itself surely is a sign of development.

A point which deserves special mention is that the local bodies over a period of time exhibited general apathy and indifference towards women's development and participation both at the general and institutional levels. Hence women's representation on these bodies has come to be symbolised by 'tokenism' and not by meaningful association. Further, women members are not treated on par with male members either by the members of the institutions or by the officials. Some of the active women members of the Zilla Parishad said that on many occasions, their views were not paid any heed only because of the fact that they are woman members. They further said that this attitude of the male members as well as the officials disillusioned them so much they were forced not to express their opinions on several occasions.

Environmental Constraints

Rural women have lesser opportunities than urban women for social gatherings. This situation creates an atmosphere of aloofness among them and does not facilitate free and unhesitating expression of views except in rare cases. Several of the women members of Gram Panchayats and Panchayat Samithis said at the time of interview that they felt delicate and shy even to sit in the meetings along with men. Apart from an atmosphere of general inhibitions, tradition in rural society prevents women from taking active roles. Some examples can be given here to illustrate this point. One woman member of the ordinary Samithi said, "the president is the elder brother of my husband. How can I sit in the meeting along with him? Does it not amount to disrespect to my brother-in-law ? Hence I will not go to meetings but will sign in the register when it is brought to my house." It should be pointed out here that women's entry into politics is socially highly objectionable until very recently. A curious instance can be given here. In the early years of the inception of the ordinary Samithi in the sample, it became very difficult for the Samithi to enlist women as members because neither women accepted membership nor men were willing to allow women to accept. But the Act was particular that women should find place on the Panchayati Raj bodies. Under such peculiar circumstances, the Samithi members could secure the willingness of two prostitutes to be on the Samithi as coopted members! It was the women whose social status was considered the lowest that were made members. But surprisingly, the same men who made these women coopted members felt insulted to sit in the meetings along with these women. As an alternative, they brought two innocent, ignorant, illiterate poor women who lost their husbands in their childhood and who were eking out their livelihood by working in the fields to this political institution and imposed on them the status of representation. This was the situation in the 60s. By the 70s, the objections for the entry of women belonging to respectable families got relaxed and the practice of choosing women coming from slightly higher status (who are either relatives or close to the president) started in the Samithi. By the 80s women with considerable interest in improving women's lot got into the same Samithi.

The fact that politics has become a rich man's profession and that women do not have independent incomes keep women away from this field even if they are interested in. The *weak economic position* of women will have a negative bearing on women's sense of confidence and vigour.

Another environmental constraint is that a majority of rural public in general and that rural women in particular do not have a reasonable idea of the principles of democratic decentralisation, popular participation and devolution of power. Further, an awareness, of a reasonable degree, of the purposes and functions of Panchayati Raj institutions does not exist in the rural scene. In this context, it is important to point out that the officials in the rural areas do not seem to adequately play the role of awareness agents. According to one study, the officials themselves felt that there is no need to enlighten about the Panchayats to the very people amidst whom they were located.

The officials also frankly admitted that they did not generally meet women for creating awareness about the institutions like Panchayats and schools. The village officials felt that they had very little to do with Mahila Mandals as these, according to them, are organisations meant for women and meant to be run only by women.[8] It was observed in another study that administrators would not like women to play a role in politics.[9] An atmosphere of distrust between officials and women exists in some villages.

Coming to the interaction between bureaucrats and women representatives, a sense of cooperation and understanding does not seem to be present. This is clear from the views expressed by some women members of the Zilla Parishad and Panchayat Samithis and Mandala Praja Parishads in the sample. A member of the erstwhile Legislative Council of Andhra Pradesh who was also the ex-officio member of the East Godavari Zilla Parishad said that it became very difficult for her to convince Collectors on important matters and that they do not pay any heed to what the women members said in the meetings. Another member, who was a coopted member expressed similar views. She said that a Collector took a very long time to get convinced that the proposal for constituting a Mahila Mandal in the heart of a village is a fair proposal.

One of the important obstacles for women's entry and participation in politics is the role-conflict. Women have to shoulder greater responsibilities than men in bringing up children and looking after household work. Negligence of household duties may even result in the break up of family ties and a political woman has to be cautious enough in striking a good balance between her role as a house-wife and as a politician.

Low educational levels and more so illiteracy are found to be directly related to low level or absence of participation among many members of rural political bodies. Several woman members said at the time of interview that their inability to participate was due to the fact that they are not educated. One woman member said, "I am anxious to participate. But I could not, because I am not educated." Another woman said "I only heard what others said and came back. I wanted to participate. I could not, because I am not educated."

STEPS FOR REVITALISATION

It has been pointed out earlier that trends of revitalisation in the context of political participation of rural women are evident and that the 'development psyche' could really be noticed in them. Another development in support of the revitalisation trend relates to the incorporation in the relevant Acts, of the provisions guaranteeing certain percentage of key positions to women in Andhra Pradesh at the Zilla and Mandal levels and reservation of 1/4 of seats for women in the middle and district level political institutions in Karnataka. In Andhra Pradesh some Zilla Praja Parishads have women as presiding officers and voters in several Mandala Praja Parishads chose women as their leaders. In Karnataka, in over 200 Zilla Parishad constituencies, men voted for women. In Madhya Pradesh, according to a report of the year 1984, 105 Panchayats chose women as the Sarpanches.[10] The recent constitutional amendment is definitely a stronger step in the direction of increasing women's participation in rural political bodies.

Another encouraging trend is that men's attitudes towards women's entry into politics have changed, though objections for active participation seem to persist. The situation moved from one of total rejection to limited objection and in some cases active encouragement too.

It is the above trend that should be strengthened and it is the women that have ability and talent that should be made to come to the forefront immediately. It is these women that should be given systematic training to lead and effectively lead. A psychological transformation in favour of active political involvement is now desired. Some suggestions could be given in this context.

Allotment of a Considerable Number of Seats to Women in the Local Bodies in General

Allotment of a considerable number of seats to women in the Gram Panchayats, Panchayat Samithis and Zilla Parishads is essential to encourage women's entry into political institutions. The presence of sufficient number of women in any association would limit their diffidence and inhibitions. As to the percentage of seats to be reserved or allotted, no uniform pattern has been adopted so far. But the proposed constitutional amendment, as mentioned earlier, provides for a uniform method of reserving 30% seats to women in all the Panchayati Raj bodies. It may not be out of place to mention that the same principle of reservation could be extended to State and Central Legislatures.

The method of reservation could be argued against on the grounds that it is against equality; it is difficult to withhold privileges once granted; other sections may also demand reservations; it breeds narrow outlooks and that the interests of women cannot be isolated from the interests of the society at large. But the point is that if the prevailing conditions are such that facilitate equal competition, the need for reservations would not arise at all. In fact, as some members of the Committee on the Status of Women felt, reservation facilitates reasonably adequate presence of women in these bodies, increases the sense of responsibility of women in the process of development and provides access to policy making. Above all it develops a sense of belongingness and confidence.

Given the barriers of equal partnership, reservation for the offices of some chair positions in all States is imperative. Under representation of women in strategic positions, particularly in local and middle level institutions as pointed out in an international seminar, would not enable women to contribute reasonably to rural development.

Provision for All-Woman Panchayats

One important way of encouraging rural women to enter politics is the constitution of All-Woman Panchayats by means of legislation. This suggestion was already made by the Committee on the Status of Women. The Committee very clearly stated that the proposed statutory women's Panchayats are not meant to be parallel organisations to the Gram Panchayats and that they are recommended as a transitional measure to break through the traditional attitudes in rural society. The Committee hoped that the working of All-Women Panchayats reduces the inhibitions of women and facilitates them to actively participate in local bodies.

It is to be noted that long before Committee's above recommendation some All-Woman Panchayats were experimented with. For example, in the 70s, Mattupalli village in the Kurnool District of Andhra Pradesh had an All-Woman Panchayat. In Vanjara, a village in Maharashtra, an All-Woman Panchayat was set up under the initiative of a local MLA. In Gandhinagaram, a village in the Hanumakonda Panchayat Samithi of Warangal district, an All-Woman

Panchayat was set up in 1981. In most cases, the All-Woman Panchayats were found to be ineffective. But this ineffectiveness is due to the absence of real motivation coupled with the consequence of manipulations by vested interests. Therefore the failure of the All-Woman Panchayats should not itself lead one to question the desirability constituting them. An attempt to understand the principle behind the setting up of these bodies and an effort to make them purposeful is presently needed.

Training

The need for training rural women has often been emphasised by analysts of social development. Presence of effective leadership facilitates organised action to solve problems and if need be through pressure tactics[13]. For the emergence of useful and responsible leadership, a systematic approach is needed. In some of the African and Asian societies, such efforts have been made and found useful. For instance, at Nisamizi in Uganda, a multipurpose training centre, two of whose objectives are to train women leaders and to train men and women community development workers has been functioning; in Guyana, women's institutions to give education to women for leadership roles exist; in Japan groups called Living Improvement Groups mainly composed of women of rural communities help to plan improvement projects, and Thailand launched community development programmes through women and youth. All these programmes are aimed to train women leaders[14]. The details of systematic programmes meant for leadership training should be carefully designed. One study found out that omission to incorporate women in training programmes, projects and schemes would reinforce inequalities[15].

Apart from training, it is important to facilitate informal discussions among women members of the local bodies at regular intervals. The officials incharge of women welfare could take a lead in this regard.

Attitudinal Change

Another important effort required is to bring about attitudinal change in both men and women. The feeling that women are meant for home should be replaced by a feeling of equal partnership. The Committee on the Status of Women pointed out that both men and women should be made to feel that women's interests cannot be isolated from general social and political interests of groups, strata and classes in the society and that women should be recognised as equals. In the absence of equality, the so-called 'sex apartheid'[16] continues for a long time to come. To prevent this, education to bring about social and political awareness should be given to men as well as women. It should be mentioned here that Women's Movement necessitated a rethinking of men's attitudes towards women. Exploitation, subordination and subservience are severely criticised and disapproved of. Teaching men about women yielded beneficial results. For example, a teaching course in the psychology of Sex Roles with special emphasis on women's role to a predominantly male audience produced tremendous difference in the outlooks of male participants. Some of the males who underwent the course felt that it had helped them to become better human beings in their interaction with females[17].

Educating men and women to bring about changes in outlooks is possible through intensification and proper use of adult educational programmes for those who are not in the process of formal education and restructuring of syllabi and its instruction to school children and college going students. An extensive use of mass media is also useful in bringing about fundamental changes. These efforts would facilitate the emergence of a new generation with new values.

Strengthening Women's Organisations

The need for women organising themselves has been emphasised by many analysts. The Ashok Mehta Committee endorsed the need for village level women's organisations and felt that they are likely to influence both directional and implementational levels. The Mahila Mandals which exist in the rural areas can be used effectively as instruments to organise and mobilise women. But unfortunately, most of the Mahila Mandals in the rural areas are dormant and very little care is taken to strengthen them as agents of encouraging women's participation in social activities. According to one study, the success of Mahila Mandals as instruments of disseminating new ideas and skills to rural women is limited because they are only adopting what is called a 'middle-class bias' and playing a 'club-like' role[18]. But within the framework of their objectives, some Mahila Mandals have proved themselves successful. The Mahila Mandals in Dhiraj village in Gujarat, Parbatpura and Gagwana villages in Rajasthan, Mukkamala and Gollapalam villages in Andhra Pradesh are examples of these.

Promotion of Income Generating Activities

The financial dependence of women, as pointed out earlier, has a negative bearing on women's sense of confidence and vigour. Hence it is necessary to involve women in large numbers in economically gainful activities. Contemporary research on women and work found that genuine effort in encouraging women's involvement in income-generating work yielded satisfactory results. For example, a cattle project in Dusan, in the Republic of Korea; rice noodles and cottage industry in Pangkal Petai in Malaysia; toys and vegetables projects in Sidhiganesh in Nepal; transportation activities in some villages of Sri Lanka; tailoring and plastic bag making in Kanchipuram in India; women's cooperatives in Indonesia and Cottage industries and training centres in some places of Bangladesh have been successfully operated with a little encouragement at the start.[19]

Another step in the direction of income-generation could be the establishment and promotion of village cooperatives to women. It can be pointed out here that a number of States in India has established statutory Women's Cooperative Finance Corporations to provide credit facilities for promising women entrepreneurs.The organi sational net-work of these corporations is spread from the state level to village level and the benefactors could be from all levels. But unfortunately, knowledge of even the existence of these corporations is limited only to a few, that too to those living in the headquarters of the States. One, therefore, need not be surprised if the benefits are obtained by men in the name of women.

Contact with People Outside Villages

Studies on women in politics stressed that education and contact with the world outside make women more alert and active in the political process. Some women members interviewed by the writer expressed similar views. There are two ways of establishing contacts between rural and urban people. One is that of facilitating exchange of views with others in the rural areas themselves, and the second is that of the urban people visiting rural areas and exchanging views with the rural people. Constant contact between the rural and urban people will reduce the rural-urban gap in orientations as well as activities.

Other Steps

For a meaningful participation of women in political roles, additional measures like appointment of women clerks to Gram Panchayats and enabling women of urban areas to become members of rural political institutions, if need be without right to vote in the meetings, would also be useful. The method of enabling urban women to become members of rural bodies could be detailed here. Urban women who originally belong to rural areas and who are willing to extend their services to rural people could be made members of the Panchayati Raj bodies.

'Let women compete and come up through reservation to actively participate in the socio-economic and political process' seems to be the accepted principle. Implementation of not merely the letter but also the spirit of law is important for women's development.

References

1. Sahul Mamie S., The Status of Women in Local Governments around the world, a Paper presented to a working group of International Union of Local Authorities, Columbus, Ohio, USA, 1981 (unpublished).
2. Shivayya M. *et al, Panchayati Raj: An Analytical Study*. p.126.
3. Mariana Githens and Prestage Jewel L. (ed) *A Portrait of Marginality: The Political Behaviour of America In Women*, Longman, New York, London, 1977, p. 5.
4. Reston James, *American Women in Public Life Today*, Peggy Lamson, Hougton, Boston, 1968, p. XXI.
5. White, Theodore H., *New Power, New Politics: The American Review*, Summer 1984, pp. 33-34.
6. See Janet A Flammang (ed) *Political Women: Current Roles in State and Local Governments*, Sage Publications, New Delhi, 1984.
7. Halef Ajshar, *Women, State and Ideology*, Macmillan, London, 1987, p. 1.
8. Mumtaz Ali Khan, Panchayati Raj and Weaker Sections of the Society: Role of Village Panchayats (Summary of Proceedings of the Panchayati Raj. Zonal Conference of Southern States held in 1976 in Bangalore). Karnataka Panchayat Parishad, Bangalore and All India Panchayat Parishad, Delhi, p. 58.
9. Kuldeep Mathur, *Bureaucratic Response to Development*, National Publishing House, New Delhi, 1972, pp. 58-59.
10. Mahila Chetna Manch, *Women and Children in Madhya Pradesh: A Profile*, Bhopal, 1985, pp. 208-217.
11. Majumdar Vina, (ed) *Role of Rural Women in Development, Report of an International Seminar*, 1978, p. 1.
12. Chandramani, G.Y., Profiles of Women in Andhra Pradesh, Vina Majumdar (ed) *Symbols of Power, op.cit.* p. 188.
13. A Report on the Workshop on Integrated Rural Development Programme and Development of Women and Children in Rural Areas, *Prajnan*. vol. XII, No.4, Oct-Dec, 1983, p. 342.
14. Secretary-General, United Nations Organisation, Report on the Participation of Women in Community Development, New York, 1972, pp. 23-25.
15. Chitra Ghosh, The Changing Status of Women in India and the ASEAN Countries: A Reflection, *Asian Studies*, Vol.I, Oct, 1983, p. 6.
16. Krishna Iyer, Women's Lot in Fact, *Voluntary Action*, Vol. 26, No.102, July-August 1983, p. 363.
17. Rehana Ghadially, *Teaching Men about Women in Women in Indian Society*, Sage Publications, New Delhi, 1988, pp. 265-69.
18. Rekha Mehra and Sarada Moni K, *Women and Rural Transformation*, Concept, New Delhi, 1982, pp. 24-25.
19. See ESCAP and FAO, Report of Inter-Country Project for the Promotion and Training of Rural Women in Income Raising Group Activities, 1979.

APPENDICES

Appendix I

Extracts from the Report of the Team for the Study of Community Projects and National Extension Service: Committee on Plans Projects (Balwant Rai Mehta Committee Report), New Delhi, November 1957 (Vol. I)
relating to women's representation in Panchayat Raj Institutions and work among women and children.

2.28. In regard to the Constitution of Panchayat, we suggest that this should be purely on an elective basis, but that there may be a provision for the cooption of two women members and one member each from the Scheduled Caste and Scheduled Tribe in conditions similar to those prescribed for the Panchayat Samithi. We do not consider that members of any other special group need any special representation either by election or by cooption.

Section 7

7.1 The Second Five Year Plan observed: "the experience gained in Social Welfare Extension Projects as well as in Community Project areas deserves to be studied more closely with the object of evolving suitable patterns of organisation for work among rural women and children. In each district, there should be close co-ordination between National Extension and Community Projects and Social Welfare Extension Projects." Nine months later, the Estimates Committee of the Parliament recommended that "an integrated programme should be drawn up for the project areas in consultation with the Central Social Welfare Board and other women's organisations." These observations confirm public apprehensions that Government funds were being spent through agencies, whose activities were unco-ordinated.

7.2. In an N.E.S. block there is only one woman S. E. O. who has to look after the welfare of the women and children of 100 villages or in an average sized block round about 45,000 persons; and at the end of three years she is, if she is lucky, given two Gram Sevikas "sometimes hardly literate", who again are withdrawn after three years. All these works she is expected to do without any transport; in the Central Social Welfare Board Projects, always located outside N.E.S. blocks, on the other hand, the Convenor of each Project implementation Committee of the C.S.W.B. possesses a jeep-intended for use in 25 villages but almost never available to the project staff. Considering that out of the total expenditure of about 90 lakhs on the various projects of the Central Social Welfare Board in the First Plan period, as much as 33 lakhs have been spent on buying jeeps alone (apart from their maintenance). We feel these jeeps could have been more profitably used jointly by the women field staff of the development blocks and the C.S.W.B. projects. Since then efforts have been made and some understanding reached between the Central Social Welfare Board and the Community Development Ministry, the two main channels for expenditure of Central Government funds in this field. The terms of agreement indicated a desire to ensure the continued existence of the two 'parties' as it were — which is rather unfortunate and does not augur well for their future activities. Six months after this agreement, in June 1957, the Chairman, Central Social Welfare Board, complained that she could not even 'get full information about the location of the community development blocks in various States'.

7.3. We feel that if our objective is to provoke and develop in rural women "progressive outlook for intelligently participating in the nation building activities" and if we have failed to do this in spite of our effort in the past six years, it is imperative that work should be directed from one point alone, and one general policy should be adopted as followed. This work is inter-related to the functions of the State Departments and Central Ministries dealing with health, village industries, education, poultry-keeping and animal husbandry; and similarly in the block and in the village to the activities of the corresponding development staff. Here again, we would like to emphasize what we saw in Section 4 about the coordination between the Central Ministries and the States. Complete responsibility for the work will be with the State and the Centre functioning as the advisory, coordinating and financing agency.

7.4. For various reasons, such as the lack of properly qualified field workers, the indefinite content of the programme and vagueness regarding the objectives, whatever little work has been done, has been confined to semi-urban areas and larger villages; and, even there, it has taken little account of the women and children belonging to the poorer sections of the community. The Estimates Committee expressed its feeling that "so far ..... rural women by and large have been left untouched. Sporadic efforts in educating village women in certain crafts and in opening some recreational centres and clubs at certain places seem to be all that has been done in that direction." Recently, the Team also , while visiting one of the States, noticed that the 'poor and backward people attended women's centres in small numbers and were attracted only to such occupations as were remunerative in the long run' and 'they were not attracted to Bhajan and Harikatha programmes.' In the Madras State Social Welfare Advisory Board Report[3] the Chairman, Mrs. Reddy observes that "in some villages the adult women do not show any interest in either learning letters or handicrafts, for the very reason that the whole time is occupied in the fields where they are engaged for the production of foodgrains and when they return home they find themselves too tired to attend evening classes at the centre outside their own homes." All this makes it abundantly clear that we have yet to redefine our objectives; and having done so, design a pattern of work and evolve suitable machinery for attaining those objectives.

7.5. At different times and in different parts of the country, stress has been laid on different aspects of welfare works like literacy, culture, health and hygiene, removal of social disabilities, beautifying of homes, women's clubs and so on. The Ministry has, however, very recently recognised that the programme for rural women must be supported by "making economic and child welfare activities . . . . . the centre around which women can continue building up their community life." (Agenda VI, Mussourie Conference). These two objectives are surely more than ample and their restricted scope indicates a sense of realism.

7.6. Even within this restricted sphere, there are a number of items which concern the community as a whole, and should, therefore, be separated while designing our pattern of work intended exclusively for women and children. For instance, the provision of drinking water or the building of sanitary latrines or construction of roads need not be the concern of the persons dealing with the women's and children's welfare; their primary concern should be to find ways in which the rural women might be assisted to increase their income and improve the condition of the children.

7.7. At present literacy is an important item in the programme for women's and children's welfare. We feel that the adult literacy programme for women above, say 25 or even 20, has no importance whatsoever; for other women also, the literacy programme, taken by itself has no appeal; for one thing they have very little leisure for book-learning; besides, such learning can hardly enrich their lives; abstract learning has very little meaning to a village woman. Equally has 'home improvement' in some of its aspects any significance to her. 'Light and Ventilation' ought to be attended to at the time of construction of the house and in the construction of the house it is the man whose voice counts; this is, therefore, not a matter where the Gram Sevika can be of much use. Beautifying the house by "arrangement and orderliness of utensils in the kitchen, the boxes, bedding etc." has been recommended. This particular recommendation is clearly unrealistic; it ignores the fact that to the larger section of the village community a house is a single-roomed hut which is the kitchen, the bed-room, the dining room and the parlour, and not unoften the cattle-shed. The number of their earthly possessions is too small to be arranged into 'orderliness.' Besides, it is not always that the rural women lack aesthetic sense in beautifying the house — the designs on the walls of their mud-huts, in some areas, have been copied by the sophisticated city women. Magan Chulha or the smokeless chulha is a good thing. But when the village woman has only one or two cooking pots and cannot afford more, it is hard to persuade her to take it. We noticed that very few of the Gram Sevikas used Magan Chulhas. It is necessary to evolve designs suitable to different areas instead of propagating one type all over the country. Health and hygiene are undoubtedly very important though it is rarely that one comes across them in a village. Here, however, the fault lies not with the programme but with the work. It appears to us that the training centres of the Gram Sevikas should stress less on the theory of sanitation than on its actual practice. In their daily lives in the training centres the urgency of personal and evironmental cleanliness should be drilled into the Gram Sevikas.

7.8. Increasingly and very rightly, the stress is shifting from providing amenities to creating work that brings more income. A few items like the care of the cow, the kitchen-garden and poultry-keeping are in the opinion of the Team, the most effective development works of the rural women. The development work will then be tangible and therefore truly lasting and will lead to welfare. The work itself is in keeping with the background of our village women, the quick and assured; it can also be easily interwoven, in the pattern of their normal daily duties. The produce can either be marketed or consumed within the family with real benefit to all, especially to the children. Incidentally, these items of work, if taken up seriously will increase the nation's supply of milk and eggs on which the Planning Commission has laid so much stress. These items should for a long time to come continue to receive the primary attention of our women workers in the villages.

7.9. After this come cottage industries which cannot always easily be interwoven into the daily pattern of the rural women's life. Only those, who have a certain amount of leisure, can be persuaded to take up one or more of them. Nor will such persuasion be useful unless they can be satisfied that what they produce will sell and fetch money. Knitting, embroidery and tailoring which are taught these days by the Gram Sevikas, as a matter of course, have, we feel, no economic possibilities, excepting in villages which are near large cities and even then, only where the work is of a high standard. These particular items appear to have been taken up mainly because of the success of the rural centres run by foreign Christian Missionaries. But we forget that such centres were limited in number, the teachers very well qualified and the performance of such excellence that the Missions could without much difficulty market all the articles both in India and abroad. On the other hand, what is necessary is to teach most of them the elementary use of thread and needle so that they can mend clothes for the family. All the same we do not say that no effort should be made to develop needle craft of knitting or even tailoring but this can be done only when a large and ready market is close by and authorities can engage really qualified and competent teachers.

7.10. In such villages as surround large towns and cities we can also start cookery classes. Women who are likely to come to the city in search of employment and then drift, would be immensely benefited by these. It should not be difficult to secure decent jobs for such trained women through the employment exchanges.

7.11. We have indicated later in this Report the points to which increasing attention has to be paid in the sphere of rural industries. Here, we would merely stress that cottage industries and the slight addition which they would make to the family income or the household income should go a considerable way in creating among our village woman a desire for economic progress in other directions.

7.12. This programme, concentrating as it does on a few points, nevertheless requires staffing with a different type of personnel than at present. Such personnel is admittedly in short supply. Also, it requires very carefull organisation and intensive supervision. We have, therefore, suggested later in this Section limiting it in extent in the next few years.

7.13. The current child welfare programme is vague and often unimaginative. Most of the work in this line has centred round what is known as the Balwadi which, in rural areas, is nearly always an anaemic creche, an unscientific kinder-garten and a jumble of different age-groups.

7.14. We feel that we have yet to evolve a satisfactory programme for our children and for this purpose, we recommend that, to begin with, we should concentrate on a few selected areas as an experimental measure. While going ahead with the right type of training for future workers, we should restrict our work to a few lines. For this purpose, the children might be grouped into four categories:

(1) Infants up to 18 months.
(2) One and a half years to three years.
(3) Three years to six years, and
(4) Six years upwards.

The health visitor and the Gram Sevika should visit every member of the first group very frequently, the former at least once a week and the latter three times a week; they should guide and assist the mother in all matters relating to the baby. Regular creches have to be started for the second and the third groups with trained staff paid for possibly by the Panchayats; these creches will serve as useful training centres for those village women who wish to take to nursing or children's work in private homes. The fourth group consisting of both boys and girls must go to school. But most of these children are away from home, grazing cattle or looking after crops. To make it possible for these also to attend school, children of each of the top three classes in the schools can be divided into two batches; each such batch can attend to grazing cattle one day in the week while the rest study. This arrangement will lead to a five day week for all these children without interfering with their field work, and this is where the Gram Sevika should be useful in persuading the village parents to send their children to school.

7.15. This limited programme which we have recommended is only the beginning, but its success depends very largely on the ability of staff to execute it. This again depends on the material we recruit to our training centres and also on the curricula. At present, according to the Expert Committee on Training "Some of the selected candidates were hardly literate." The candidate working in the projects of the Central Social Welfare Board are not different in calibre. We have to choose between reasonable standard of quality with the inevitable limits of quantity on the one hand and a vast unenlightened quantity on the other. The costly experience of the past few years should help us to decide. We feel that it will be useful and easy to recruit Gram

Sevikas from amongst matriculate teachers working in the rural or semi-rural areas. They will necessairly have to be given a special or a higher scale of pay as an inducement.

7.16. The present curriculum is, in our opinion, unrelated to reality. Few of our Gram Sevikas will find useful the items mentioned in that curriculum beginning with 'what food does for us' and going through 'the fibres commonly used for clothing and how to identify them, distinguishing silk, rayon, cotton, wool, artificial silk, etc.' and going up to 'the household medicine box and simple remedies like aspirin, argyrol, sulfa guanadine etc.' This curriculum apparently based on foreign conception needs to be revised and made to suit our rural conditions. We shall further discuss this matter in a later section.

7.17. According to the C.S.W.B. pattern a group of about 25 villages is served by 5 Gram Sevikas, 5 craft teachers, 5 dais and one Mukhya Sevika for a period of three years, apart from the office staff. This works out at 20 Gram Sevikas, 20 craft teachers, 20 dais and 4 Mukhya Sevikas per block in addition to four times the office staff. In the N.E.S. pattern, there is a woman S.E.O. for one block of about 100 villages and after three years she is given the assistance of 2 Gram Sevikas who are withdrawn after another three years.

7.18. In the block-projects started after the agreement between the C.S.W.B. and the Ministry of Community Development, there are 10 Gram Sevikas, 2 craft instructresses, 8 part-time workers in charge of Balwadis and 5 dais; in addition, there are 6 supervisory persons apart from the woman S.E.O.

7.19. We have already recommended that the number of Gram Sevaks should be raised to about 20 per block. It will be necessary to have at least an equal number of Gram Sevikas, whose recruitment and training we shall indicate later, working full time. We do not consider that it is necessary to continue the woman S.E.O. as at present. Instead, we suggest that there should be a Mukhya Sevika who would be selected from amongst the Gram Sevikas on the basis of merit alone, and if necessary given a little extra training in particular lines. All of them will be guided by the block-level extension officers in health, industries, education, animal husbandry, etc. Some of the craft instructresses' posts should, in our opinion, be abolished and the others integrated with the staffing pattern for rural industries so that we will be able to employ good craftsmen to teach both men and women and look after the progress of the village industry. The Gram Sevikas will assist them in their work among women. The dais or such of them as will be needed, as also the health visitor and the midwife can be integrated with and enlarge the staff of the primary health centres and sub-centres. The welfare programme amongst women and children is not to be a temporary affair and has to occupy a permanent place in our socialistic pattern of society; the staff appointed for it should, therefore, be made permanent; with a sense of security the quality of their work should improve. Obviously, they can only work as employees either of the State Government or of a statutory local body.

7.20. We are suggesting that community development should be planned and carried out in phases of six years which need not be sub-divided as at present into what are known as the N.E.S. and C.D. stages. This will also apply to the programme for women and children. The programme which we have suggested requires a well qualified and well trained personnel; if only because such personnel is scarce we must limit the scope of our present activities; we suggest that one block should be selected in each district and it should be near the district or sub-divisional headquarters so that it can receive the maximum attention from senior officers as also from women's voluntary organisations. No work in a block should be started until there is the full complement of trained personnel. Only after these blocks have shown results, should the programme be extended to other blocks.

7.21. As already pointed out, most of the C.S.W.B. projects are outside the community development block areas. The existing projects should be forthwith transferred to the State Governments which should arrange for their administration and supervision either through departmental agencies or through local statutory bodies.

Appendix II

Extracts from the report of the Ashok Mehta Committee (1978), relating to the role of women in Panchayati Raj

Role of Women

X. 9 In developing and harmonising the human resources in developmental endeavours, the most important part of our population needs special discussion. Out of 264 million female population, 214 million live in rural areas. Of 31 million women at work, 28 million were in rural areas. According to 1971 Census, it is the vast resources which is already contributing richly to rural economic development that has to be given a greater role in the Panchayati Raj Institutions.

X. 10.1 The involvement of rural women in the developmental process has always been regarded as an integral part of the total development of the village community. The introduction of Panchayati Raj has added another dimension to the role of rural women. Their role in decison-making on development project has been brought to fore-front. The Committee on the Status of Women in India has even suggested establishment of statutory women's panchayats at the village level. The proposal emanates from the postulate that their contribution to the rural economy has not been adequately appreciated and if appreciated has not been institutionalised; that their representation in Panchayati Raj Institutions is mainly 'token' and not effective in articulating women's needs or for mobilising their adequate participation. These two aspects of a voice in decision-making and participation in the elective process are in a way related. Greater representation of women in the Panchayati Raj bodies and participation in the elective process are in a way related and likely to influence both the directional and the implementational level.

X. 10.2 With regard to participation in elections, part of the idea in the Punjab Panchayat Samithis and Zilla Parishads Act, 1961, would be relevant. The Act provides that two women securing the highest number of votes amongst the women candidates in the election, take the seats reserved for them. This is a method of co-option by election.

The Committee would support such a procedure. It is further suggested that these seats be in addition to the general seats which they may win by a majority in the normal course. Thus, women can possibly get more seats than reserved. This appears to be a convenient mode of securing adequate participation of women in Panchayati Raj elections.

X. 10.3 Further, an institutional arrangement through a Committee with all women members of the Mandal Panchayat represented on it would also ensure that decisions are made by women themselves on priorities and choices in welfare and development programmes specifically for women and children. In the process of modernisation of agriculture, in the commercialisation of activities allied to agriculture, in accenting mobility of labour, often the special difficulties of women are lost sight of, and as a result they become losers through development. Care has to be taken to prepare programmes suited to their needs during the transition phase. Such Committee should have the powers of the Panchayat, with reference to the money for the programmes being specifically earmarked for them.

X. 10.4 Growing emphasis on rural industrialisation will also necessitate women's active participation and involvement in achieving the desired diversification of occupational pattern in the rural areas. These industries with varying levels of technology, skills of production can provide gainful employment to rural woman. It will be desirable that institutional finance and budgetary support for programmes meant in these areas are designed for these groups in the plan suggestions and formulation at Mandal and District levels. Arrangements may have to be made to ensure that financial assistance in the shape of loan is sanctioned to women beneficiaries.

X. 11 The organisation of Mahila Mandals has been one of the components in the rural development programmes. Recently, the need to integrate the programme for rural women with Integrated Rural Development has been emphasized. The 'new' programme for rural women should recognise and strengthen their constructive, decision-making and managerial roles so as to enable them to have full access to development resources and services. The motivational and promotional role of Panchayati Raj will be crucial in this area.

Appendix III

Extracts from Towards Equality (Report of the Committee on the Status of Women, 1974) relating to reservation of seats for women in local bodies and the establishment of statutory women's panchayats at the village level to ensure greater participation of women in the political process.

7.115 Even though we did not accept the suggestions for reservation for women in Parliament or the State Legislature, we find that in order to provide greater opportunites to women to actively participate in the decision-making process, it is imperative to recognise the true nature of the social inequalities and disabilities that hamper them. This can best be achieved by providing them with special opportunities for participation in the representative structures of local Government. The necessity to associate women representatives in local self-governing bodies is already accepted in this country and provision for reservation of seats for women through either election, co-option or nomination in these bodies exist in most of the state legislations that govern the constitution of these bodies.

7.116 It has been our experience, however, that this association, with the exception of a few areas is mostly regarded as a form of 'tokenism'. We feel that the time has come now to move out of this token provision for women's representation to a more meaningful association of women in the structure of local administration.

A second reason for this is the general apathy and indifference of these local bodies of women's development and change of status which has been reported to us by women's organisations and welfare and extension workers, particularly in rural areas. It may be noted that a large number of Mahila Mandals have been organised in both rural and urban areas through the initiative of welfare organisations like the Central Social Welfare Board and its state agencies, Ministry of Agriculture and Community Development and voluntary bodies like the Bharatiya Grameen Mahila Sangh. The status of these bodies is purely voluntary. Some of their members have acquired both experience and interest in developmental activities, but they are not representatives and their constitution does not result in associating or involving large majority of women in these activities. Nor do these bodies receive much recognition from the statutory local self-governing institutions. We received complaints of neglect and lack of funds for women's programmes from women workers throughout the country. This was confirmed by specialists working in the field of Community Development and Panchayati Raj.

7.117 *We therefore recommend the establishment of Statutory Women's Panchayats at the village level to ensure greater participation by women in the political process.* These bodies are not meant to be parallel organisations to the Gram Panchayats but should form an integral part of the Panchayati Raj structure, with autonomy and resources of their own for the management and administration of welfare and development programmes for women and children. We recommend them as a transitional measure to break through the traditional attitudes in rural society which inhibit most women from articulating their problems or participating actively in the existing local bodies. An exclusively women's body would eliminate this difficulty and provide opportunity to more women to gain experience and confidence in managing their own affairs. Their enhanced legal status, we believe, will have a direct impact on the general status of women in rural society and their increasing experience and responsibility may be expected to improve women's keenness and capacity for greater participation in the political process. Lastly, the existence of such statutory bodies would help to ensure better co-ordination of various Government services and programmes for women at the level of implementation. Like the Panchayats, these bodies could be directly elected by the women of the village and should have the right to send their representatives to the Panchayat Samities and/or Zilla Parishads. To ensure a viable relationship between the existing Gram Panchayats and the proposed women's panchayats, the Chairman and Secretary of both these bodies should be ex-officio members of the other.

2. At the level of municipalities the principle of reservation of seats for women is already prevalent in certain States. *We therefore recommend that this should be adopted by all States as a transitional measure.**

We also recommend the constitution of permanent committees in municipalities to initiate and supervise programmes for women's welfare and development.

3. We recommend that political parties should adopt a definite policy regarding the percentage of women candidates to be sponsored by

them for elections to Parliament and State Assemblies. While they may initially start with 15%, this should be gradually increased so that in time to come the representation of women in the Legislative Bodies has some relationship to their position in the total population of the country or the state.

4. We further recommend the inclusion of women in all important committees, commissions or delegations that are appointed to examine socio-economic problems.

Appendix IV

Extracts from National Perspective Plan for Women 1988-2000 (A.D.) relating to political participation of women with special reference to Panchayati Raj bodies and recommendations of National Perspective Plan

Women in Local Government

16. The concept of participatory development, the importance of intermediaries e.g. voluntary action groups and educational institutions were recognized as important instruments to achieve the developmental goals for women. Participatory development through group organizations has been successfully attempted in several innovative projects carried out by women's organizations. The contribution of the voluntary organizations has been considered as particularly significant in demonstrating the effectiveness of participatory development as a process of empowering women to articulate their needs, to take part in decision making and in following their own vision. In this regard, the participation of women in the Panchayati Raj institutions, which were considered to be the most effective instruments for realizing the goals of economic betterment and social justice for the least privileged, was felt essential. The CSWI report suggested the establishment of all-women panchayats at village level, with autonomy and resources of their own for the management and administration of welfare and development programmes for women and children, as a transitional measure to break through the traditional attitudes that inhibit most women in articulating their problems or participating actively in the local bodies. The Empowered committee, while examining the recommendations, suggested that the sub-committee, while examining the subjects relating to management and administration of programmes for women and children should have the power of panchayat with earmarked funds.

17. Participation of women in Panchayati Raj institutions has been recognized as a step towards equality. The Committee on the Panchayati Raj institutions, 1978 recommended the reservation of two seats for women in panchayats and to co-opt women in case they did not come through elections. It also suggested that a Committee of women be set up within panchayats to operate specific programmes for women and children. The co-option of two women memebrs in panchayats, has not brought any perceptible impact on women's participation in the Panchayati Raj bodies. Co-option is done only in letter and not in the spirit of getting the women involved in panchayat activities. The participation of women in panchayats as it is today hardly gives any scope for women members to participate effectively and independently in democratic and political processes or to influence decision making.

18. The Minister of Agriculture, in a recent circular to the State Governments, asked the States to take measures for increasing effective representation of women in panchayats. The examples of Karnataka and Andhra Pradesh have been cited where 25 per cent and 30 per cent seats respectively have been reserved for women. Enhanced representation is likely to remove the isolation of women and give them visibility and strength to be more assertive and to take part in decision making.

Recommendations

7.1 It has been observed through various studies, that education of citizens not only builds up knowledge and information but also helps the citizen understand the complexities of the political process. It is, therefore, recommended that the programme of free universal education upto the age of 14 should be vigorously implemented. Further, serious attention needs to be paid to the content of education. The courses of studies and the textbooks should inculcate values of gender equality, self-respect, courage, independence etc., which would help develop the personalities of women.

7.2 In order that women are able to participate fully, it is necessary to spread legal literacy not only among the general community, but also among elected representatives. Modules can be included in existing non-formal educational programmes for this purpose.

7.3 The working of international events, the inter-relationship of various systems of society, implications of political actions and policies, economic and other such issues need to be highlighted to women.

7.4 Men and women in positions of power should be sensitized to women's issues.

7.5 Government should effectively secure participation of women in decision making processes at National, State and local levels. This would imply use of special measures for recruitment of women candidates :

* More women need to be inducted in ministries at the centre and in state governments and they must be allowed to function in areas suitable to their capacities and not be restricted to 'soft' sectors.
* The Planning Commission and all ministries and government departments must have a Women's Cell.
* All government delegations to international meetings must include at least one or more women members.
* Wherever a Committee or Commission is set up by Government for any purpose 30 per cent of its representation must be of women.
* The Union and all State level Public Service Commissions must have women represențaives.
* The Planning Commission and State Planning Boards must have adequate representation of women.
* 50 per cent of all grassroots functionaries must be women. To facilitate its implementation, relaxation of minimum educational qualifications is needed, which can be supplemented by short training courses for women.
* Reservation should be made of 30 per cent seats at panchayat to zilla parishad level and local municipal bodies for women. Wherever possible, higher representation of dalits/tribals, women of weaker sections should be ensured.
* 30 per cent of executive heads of all bodies from village panchayat to district level and a certain per centage of chief executives of panchayati raj bodies at lower, middle and higher levels must be reserved for women.
* A more effective step would be to declare a certain parcentage of constituencies in the lower tier of panchayati raj as exclusively women's constituencies and all executive positions in a certain number of territorial jurisdictions reserved for women candidates.

7.6 All women members of panchayats and other executive bodies must be trained and empowered to exercise their authority. Both men and women members must be sensitized to women's issues. A committee should be formed to look into the training needs of women panchayat members and to help in designing modules separate allocations may be made for this purpose. Particular attention must be paid to the development of interpersonal communication skills amongst the trainees/community leaders.

7.7 Conscious efforts are needed to elicit participation of women through establishing links between the elected representatives and the development functionaries as being experimented in Rajasthan through the Women's Development Programmes (WDP). The whole experiment is based on a decentralized administrative structure. Plans of action should be formulated through frequent meetings and discussions. Further the prime need is to see that the representatives have to be made answerable to the electorate. WDPs in other States must also be linked with panchayat/local functionaries for more effective participation of women in development.

7.8 Standing Advisory Committees at Central, State, District, Block and wherever possible at village level should be formed consisting of representatives of important women's organizations.

7.9 Executive bodies of trade unions must include more women.

7.10 One of the greatest hurdles in contesting elections is the exhorbitant expenditure. This factor not only makes it difficult for women, who have very limited independent resources to participate, but completely eliminates women in the poverty sector from entering the arena. This situation leads to prominence of upper castes, upper classes, urban women in the political sphere. To counteract this inequitous situation serious steps must be taken to reduce election expenditure. Further, enormous amounts needed for election lead to corruption and various nefarious practices. If steps are taken to decentralize the political machinery, then unnecessary expenditure in reaching out to a very large electorate could be avoided.

7.11 A major step needed to facilitate women's participation both in formal and informal political processes is provision of support services. In all kinds of public participation as well as in seeking opportunities for self-development, the primary responsibilities of women for looking after home and children always come in the way. Unless arrangements are made for child care and other domestic responsibilities, sustained participation of women in the public sphere is not possible without the integration of men in the private sphere. This not only means that men share the familial responsibilities but a new value needs to be given to this joint sharing both in public and private spheres which would ultimately lead to a better quality of life.

7.12 In a democracy political parties have a very significant role to play. The parties should take such measures which would facilitate participation of women. All political parties must be urged to ensure that at least 30 per cent of the candidates fielded for election are women till such time as women can stake their claim to nomination as equals. It should be examined if the Election Commision can be empowered to enforce this.

7.13 It is the bounden duty of political parties to provide political education to the people. They should organize study circles in which not only political understanding of the complex situations is provided, but controversial issues having implications on gender relations is also analysed.

7.14 Women members of the political groups should be vigilant about their rights and contributions. Whenever sexist attitudes are exhibited or sex discrimination is practised, women memebrs should build up solidarity and oppose such practices. They should also press for implementing whatever has been promised to women: whether the question is of allocation of seats or of providing a creche or taking a stand in Parliament.

7.15 In generating a participatory political system, the role of voluntary organizations or non-governmental organizations is very crucial. There is evidence that when NGOs are active and play the role of pressure goups the representatives also become alert. Through raising the awareness of the community, NGOs can help in fielding candidates who are responsible to the people. They can focus the attention of the people on crucial issues facing women and elect members who understand those issues and are working towards it. Organizations and Grassroots women's groups have in fact effectively drawn the attention of the government to atrocities perpetrated on women, to custodial rape, to harassments for dowry, to plight of the women in the unorganized sector, and so on NGOs can also provide training for future women leaders. They can organize legal literacy programmes and study circles for political education as well as develop participatory methods of working and thus serve as a practical training centre for effective political participation by women. They should not adopt a beneficiary or 'welfare' approach while working with their target groups. Even if a few NGOs play their role adequately and with courage, a new climate of commitment and responsibility could be generated.

7.16 NGOs should work as pressure groups or political action groups to press for the fulfilment of promises. They should also provide support to the elected women representatives when they are presenting women's cases in the deliberative bodies. In short there should be a very strong link between women representatives and those organizations working with the community.

7.17 Media should play a productive role in enhancing women's participation. It should give wider coverage to various activities and measures taken by women and should highlight the problems of women. In order to project women's issues and achievements, perhaps mainstream media may not be adequate and therefore, it is necessary to develop an alternate media system that could portray women's struggles and experiences, help generate values which encourage gender equality and justice and build up a positive image of women participating in public life.

7.18 For politicization of women networking and creation of pressure groups representing genuine issues and felt needs are essential.

7.19 A massive awareness campaign aimed at eliciting the support of electors (both male and female) around causes will have to be undertaken.

Appendix V

Text of the Constitution (Sixty-Fourth) Amendment Bill, 1989 as Introduced in Lok Sabha on 15 May 1989

Bill No. 50 of 1989

THE CONSTITUTION (SIXTY-FOURTH AMENDMENT) BILL, 1989

A
BILL

further to amend the Constitution of India.

BE it enacted by Parliament in the Fortieth Year of the Republic of India as follows:

1. (1) This Act may be called the Constitution (Sixty-fourth Amendment) Act, 1989.
   (2) It shall come into force on such date as the Central Government 5 may, by notification in the Official Gazette, appoint.

2. After Part VIII of the Constitution , the following Part shall be inserted, namely:

PART IX

THE PANCHAYATS

243. In this Part, unless the context otherwise requires, —
(a) "district" means a revenue district in a State;
(b) "intermediate level" means a level between the village and district levels specified by the Governor of a State by public notification to be the intermediate level for the purposes of this Part;

(5)The Chairperson of —
(a) a Panchayat at the village level shall be chosen by election in

such manner as the Legislature of the State may, by law, provide; and

(b) a Panchayat at the intermediate or district level shall be elected by, and from amongst, the elected members thereof.

(6) Where the Chairperson of a Panchayat has been elected by, and from amongst, the elected members of the Panchayat, no resolution by the Panchayat for removing him from the office of the Chairperson shall be valid and effective unless such resolution has been passed by a majority of the total number of the elected members of the Panchayat and by a majority of not less than two-thirds of such members present and voting.

243C. (1) Seats shall be reserved for the Scheduled Castes and the Scheduled Tribes in every Panchayat and the number of seats so reserved shall bear, as nearly as may be, the same proportion to the total number of seats to be filled by direct election in that. Panchayat as the population of the Scheduled Castes in that Panchayat area or of the Scheduled Tribes in the Panchayat area bears to the total population of that area:

Provided that where the population of the Scheduled Castes or, as the case may be, the Scheduled Tribes in a Panchayat area is not sufficient for reservation of any seat, one seat for the Scheduled Castes or, as the case may be, one seat for the Scheduled Tribes shall be reserved in that Panchayat.

(2) As nearly as may be, thirty per cent of the total number of seats reserved under clause (1) shall be reserved for women belonging to the Scheduled Castes or, as the case may be, the Scheduled Tribes:

Provided that where only two seats are reserved for the Scheduled Castes or, as the case may be, the Scheduled Tribes, one of the two seats shall be reserved for women belonging to the Scheduled Castes or, as the case may be, the Scheduled Tribes.

(3) Nothing in this Part shall prevent the Legislature of a State from providing for the reservation of the office of Chairpersons in the Panchayats for the Scheduled Castes, the Scheduled Tribes and women.

(4) The reservation of seats under clause (1) and clause (2) and the reservation of office of Chairpersons (other than the reservation for women) referred to in clause (3), if any, shall have effect till the expiration of the period specified in article 334 and the proviso there to shall, so far as may be, apply to such reservations.

(5) As nearly as may be, thirty per cent (including the number of seats reserved for women belonging to the Scheduled Castes and the Scheduled Tribes) of the total number of seats to be filled by direct

election in every Panchayat shall be reserved for women and allotted by rotation to diffrent constituencies in a Panchayat.

243D. (1) Every Panchayat, unless sooner dissolved under any law for the time being in force, shall continue for five years from the date appointed for its first meeting and no longer and the expiration of the said period of five years shall operate as a dissolution of that Panchayat.

(2) Where a Panchayat is dissolved before the expiration of its duration, an election to constitute the Panchayat shall be completed, as soon as may be and in any case before the expiration of a period of six months from the date of such dissolution.

(3) A Panchayat constituted upon the dissolution of a Panchayat before the expiration of its duration shall continue only for the remainder of the period for which the dissolved Panchayat would have continued under clause (1) had it not been so dissolved and, if such period is less than six months, it shall not be necessary to hold any election under clause (2) for constituting the Panchayat.

243E. Subject to the provisions of this Constitution, the Legislature of a State may, by law, endow the Panchayats with such powers and authority as may be necessary to enable them to function as institutions of self-government and such law may contain provisions for the devolution of powers and responsibilities upon Panchayats at the appropriate level, subject to such conditions as may be specified therein, with respect to :

(a) the preparation of plans for economic development and social justice;

(b) the implementation of schemes for economic development and social justice as may be entrusted to them including those in relation to the matters listed in the Eleventh Schedule.

243F. The Legislature of a State may, by law,—

(a) authorise a Panchayat to levy, collect and appropriate such taxes, duties, tolls and fees in accordance with such procedure and subject to such limits;

(b) assign to a Panchayat such taxes, duties, tolls and fees levied and collected by the State Government for such purposes and subject to such conditions and limits;

(c) provide for making such grants-in-aid to the Panchayats from the Consolidated Fund of the State; and

(d) provide for constitution of such Funds for crediting all

moneys received, respectively, by or on behalf of the Panchayats and also for the withdrawal of such moneys therefrom, as may be specified in the law.

243G. (1) The Governor of a State shall, as soon as may be within two years from the commencement of the Constitution (Sixty-fourth Amendment) Act, 1989, and thereafter at the expiration of every fifth year, constitute a Finance Commission to review the financial position of the Panchayats and to make recommendations to the Governor as to—

(a) the principles which should govern—

(i) The determination of the taxes, duties, tolls and fees which may be assigned to, or appropriated by, the Panchayats;

(ii) The distribution between the State and the Panchayats of the net proceeds of the taxes, duties, tolls and fees which are to be, or may be, divided between them under this Part and the allocation between the Panchayats at all levels of their respective shares of such proceeds;

(iii) the grants-in-aid to the Panchayats from the Consolidated Fund of the State;

(b) any other matter referred to the Finance Commission by the Governor in the interest of sound finance of the Panchayats.

(2) The Legislature of a State may, by law, determine the qualifications which shall be requisite for appointment as members of the Commission and the manner in which they shall be selected.

(3) The Commission shall determine their procedure and shall have such powers in the performance of their functions as the Legislature of the State may, by law, confer on them.

(4) The Governor shall cause every recommendation made by Finance Commission under this article together with an explanatory memorandum as to the action taken thereon to be laid before the Legislature of the State.

243H. (1) The accounts of the Panchayats shall be kept in such form as the Governor may, on the advice of the Comptroller and Auditor-General of India, prescribe.

(2) The Comptroller and Auditor-General of India shall cause the accounts of the Panchayats to be audited in such manner as he may deem fit and the reports of the Comptroller and Auditor-General shall be submitted to the Governor of the State, who shall cause them to be laid before the Legislature of the State.

243I. The superintendence, direction and control of the

preparation of electoral rolls for, and the conduct of, all elections to the Panchayats shall be vested in the Election Commission.

243J. Subject to the provisions of this Part, the Legislature of a State may, from time to time, by law, make provision with respect to all matters relating to, or in connection with, elections to the Panchayats including the preparation of electoral rolls, the manner in which the electoral rolls for the time being in force for the territorial constituencies referred to in Article 325 may be used for such preparation, the delimitation of constituencies and all other matters necessary for securing the due constitution of such Panchayats.

243K. (1) The provisions of this Part shall apply to the Union Territories and shall, in their application to a Union Territory, have effect as if the references to the Governor of a State were references to the Administrator of the Union territory appointed under Article 239 and references to the Legislature or the Legislative Assembly of a State were references, in relation to a Union Territory having a Legislative Assembly, to that Legislative Assembly.

(2) Notwithstanding anything in clause (1), the President may by public notification, direct that the provisions of this Part shall not apply to any Union Territory or any part thereof or shall apply to any Union Territory or part thereof subject to such exceptions and modifications as he may specify in the notification.

243L. (1) Nothing in this Part shall apply to—

(a) the States of Nagaland, Meghalaya and Mizoram;

(b) the Scheduled Areas referred to in clause (1), and the Tribal Areas referred to in clause (2), of article. 244;

(c) the Hill Areas in the State of Manipur for which District Councils exist, and the Hill Areas of the District of Darjeeling in the State of West Bengal for which the Darjeeling Gorkha Hill Council exists, under any law for the time being in force.

(2) Notwithstanding anything in this Constitution,—

(a) the Legislature of a State referred to in sub-clause (a) of clause (1) may, by law, extend this Part to that State, except the tribal areas, if any, referred to in sub-clause (b) of clause (1), if the Legislative Assembly of that State passes a resolution to that effect by a majority of the total membership of that House and by a majority of not less than two-thirds of the members of that House present and voting;

(b) the Governor of a State may, in his discretion and subject to such exceptions and modifications as he may specify by public notification, extend this Part to the Scheduled Areas, referred to in clause (1) of article 244, comprised within that State.

243M. Notwithstanding anything in this Part, any provision of any law relating to Panchayats in force immediately before the commencement of the Constitution (Sixty-fourth Amendment) Act, 1989, which is inconsistent with the provisions of this Part, shall continue to be in force until amended or repealed by a competent Legislature or other competent authority or until the expiration of one year from such commencement, whichever is earlier :

Provided that all the Panchayats existing immediately before such commencement shall continue till the expiration of their duration, unless sooner dissolved by a resolution passed to that effect by the Legislative Assembly of that State or, in the case of a State having a Legislative Council, by each House of the Legislature of that State.

(3) After the Tenth Schedule to the Constitution, the following Schedule shall be added, namely—

ELEVENTH SCHEDULE

(Article 243E)

1. Agriculture, including agricultural extension.
2. Land improvement and soil conservation.
3. Minor irrigation, water management and watershed development.
4. Animal husbandry, dairying and poultry.
5. Fisheries.
6. Social forestry and farm forestry.
7. Minor forest produce.
8. Small scale industries, including food processing industries.
9. Khadi, village and cottage industries.
10. Rural housing.
11. Drinking water.
12. Fuel and fodder.
13. Roads, culverts, bridges, ferries, waterways and other means of communication.
14. Rural electrification, including distribution of electricity.
15. Non-conventional energy sources.
16. poverty-alleviation programmes.
17. Education, including primary and secondary schools.
18. Technical training and vocational education.
19. Adult and non-formal education.
20. Libraries.
21. Cultural activities.
22. Markets and fairs.

23. Health and sanitation, including hospitals, primary health centres and dispensaries.
24. Family welfare
25. Women and child development.
26. Social welfare, including welfare of the handicapped and mentally retarded.
27. Welfare of the weaker sections, and in particular, of the Scheduled Castes and the Scheduled Tribes.
28. Public distribution system.
29. Maintenance of community assets.

STATEMENT OF OBJECTS AND REASONS

A review of the working of Panchayati Raj Institutions has shown that in many States they have become weak and ineffective owing to a variety of reasons, including the failure to hold regular and periodical elections, prolonged supersessions, inadequate representation to the weaker sections like the Scheduled Castes, the Scheduled Tribes and women, lack of financial resources and inadequate devolution of powers and responsibilities on them.

2. Having regard to the inadequacies in the existing system, and keeping in view the Directive Principle of State Policy enshrined in Article 40 which aims at endowing Panchayats with such powers and authority as are necessary to enable them to function as units of self-government, it is proposed to add a new Part to the Constitution relating to the Panchayats.

3. The Bill proposes, *inter alia*, to—

(a) make it obligatory for all States to establish a three-tier system of Panchayats at the village, intermediate and district levels; however, States having a population of less than 20 lakhs would not be obliged to establish Panchayats at the intermediate level;

(b) provide for all seats in Panchayats at all levels to be filled by direct election: however, the State Legislatures may provide for the representation in Panchayats without voting rights of Members of the House of the People and of the Legislative Assembly, and Chairpersons of Panchayats at the immediately lower level;

(c) provide for reservations to ensure the due representation in the Panchayats of the Scheduled Castes, Scheduled Tribes and women;

(d) ensure a fixed tenure of five years for the panchayats. However, if a Panchayat is dissolved before the expiry of its term, provision is made for the conduct of elections within a period of six months of the dissolution to reconstitute the Panchayat for the remainder of the term;

(e) provide for the devolution by the State Legislature of powers and responsibilities upon the Panchayats with respect to the preparation of plans for economic development and social justice and for the implementation of development schemes;

(f) Provide for the sound finance of the Panchayats by securing authorisation from State Legislatures for grant-in-aid to the Panchayats from the Consolidated. Fund of the State, as also assignment to or appropriation by, the Panchayats of the revenues of designated taxes, duties, tolls and fees;

(g) provide for the constitution of Finance Commissions in the States every five years to review the finances of the Panchayats and recommend principles on the basis of which State Legislatures may determine the taxes to be appropriated by, or assigned to the Panchayats, as also grants-in-aid to the Panchayats from the Consolidated Fund of the State;

(h) vest in the Election Commission the superintendence, direction and control of elections to the Panchayats at all three levels;

(i) empower the Comptroller and Auditor-General of India to cause the accounts of the Panchayats audited in such manner as he may deem fit; and

(j) exempt certain States and tribal areas and other Territories from the application of the provisions of Part IX or empower the President and the Governor to modify them in their application to Union Territories and Scheduled Areas, respectively.

4. The Bill seeks to achieve the aforesaid objectives.

NEW DELHI;
The 12th May, 1989. RAJIV GANDHI.

FINANCIAL MEMORANDUM

Clause 2 of the Bill seeks to insert new Part IX in the Constitution consisting of Articles 243 to 243M.

2. Articles 243E and 243F envisage the discharge of greater responsibility by the Panchayati Raj Institutions. This will call for strengthening the administrative capability and training requirements of the Panchayati Raj Institution at various levels. Though the responsibility in this regard is of the State Governments, the Central Government may be required to share the burden as the States' resources are not adequate. It is, however, difficult to estimate the annual recurring expenditure on account of additional staff to be created at various levels as this will require a detailed study of the existing staff strength in different States.

3. Article 243H provides for auditing of accounts of the Panchayats in such manner as the Comptroller and Auditor-General of India deems necessary. Similarly, Article 243-I provides for superintendence, direction and control of elections to the Panchayats to be vested in the Election Commission. These provisions are likely to increase the work in the office of the Comptroller and Auditor-General as well as in the Election Commission necessitating augmentation of their staff. However, both the Comptroller and Auditor-General and the Chief Election Commissioner have indicated that it would be difficult for them at present moment to estimate the likely increase in staff and the consequent financial burden without detailed study of the additional work involved. There will be no other recurring or non-recurring expenditure.

Appendix VI

Extracts from the Andhra Pradesh mandala Praja Parishads, Zilla Praja Parishads and Zilla Pranalika Abhivrudhi Sameeksha Mandals Act, 1986 as amended by Act 3 of 1987 relating to reservation of the offices of President for Women and to the representation of women on the Committee on Women Welfare

5 (2). Provided also that nine per cent of the total number of offices of President in a district [excluding the number of offices reserved under clause (a) of the second proviso] shall be reserved by the District Collector, by rotation, for women in the manner prescribed; so, however that the Mandal in respect of which the Office of President is so reserved shall as far as practicable, be the Mandal where the proportion of the population of women to the total population of the Mandal is the largest:

44 (1) provided also the nine per cent of the total number of offices of Chairman in the State shall be reserved by the Government, by rotation, from term to term, for women in the manner prescribed; so however that not more than one office of Chairman is reserved in each of the three regions of the State consisting of Coastal Andhra, Telangana and Rayalaseema and the district in respect of which the office of Chairman is so reserved shall, as far as practicable, be the district where the proportion of the population of the women to the total population of the district is the largest:

51. **Standing Committees of a Zilla Praja Parishad —** (1) For every Zilla Praja parishad there shall be constituted the following Standing Committees, the subjects assigned to each such Standing Committee being those specified against it, namely —

(i) **Standing Committee for Development —** Planning, Food and Agriculture including irrigation, wells, animal husbandry reclamation including soil conservation, contour bunding forests and fisheries, Co-operation, thrift and small savings, Industries including cottage, village and small scale industries, trust, rural housing and statistics;

(ii) **Standing Committee for Education —** Education including

Social Education, Medical relief, public health and sanitation including drainage, relief, of distress in grave emergencies and self-help progremme;

(iii) **Standing Committee for Social Welfare** — Social Welfare, welfare of Scheduled Castes, Scheduled Tribes and Backward Classes and cultural affairs:

(iv) **Standing Committee for Women Welfare** — Welfare of Women and Children;

(v) **Standing Commitee for Works** — Communication, rural water supply, power and irrigation excluding irrigation wells;

(vi) **Standing Committee for Finance** — Taxation and Finance and Co-ordination of the work relating to all other Standing Committees.

(2) (a) Every Standing Committee shall consist of the Chairman of Zilla Praja Parishad and the District Collector, who shall be ex-Officio member, and such number of members as may be arrived at by dividing the total number of members of the Parishad by six:

Provided that each of the surplus number of members, if any, remaining after such division shall be allocated to such Standing Committee as the Parishad may decide.

(b) The members of the Standing Committee shall be elected by the members of the Parishad from among themselves in the manner prescribed:

provided that atleast one representative of the Scheduled Castes or Scheduled Tribes or Backward Classes or minorities or women shall be elected to each of the Standing Committees other than the Standing Committees for Social Welfare or as the case may be, Women Welfare:

Provided further that where the total number of members of the Parishad belonging to the Scheduled Castes, Scheduled Tribes, Backward Classes and minorities, and women members is not sufficient to provide representation in every standing Committee as aforesaid or where the number of such members on the Parishad is sufficent to provide such representation, but yet a member belonging to the Scheduled Castes or Scheduled Tribes or Backward Classes or minorities or women member, is not elected to any Standing Committee for any other reason, such number of persons as are required to provide one representative in every Standing Committee shall be elected from among the Scheduled Castes or Scheduled Tribes or Backward Classes or minorities or women, as the case may be, who are registered voters in the district but not members of the Parishads:

Appendix VII

Extracts from the rules relating to reservation of offices of president of Mandala Praja Parishads and chairman of Zilla Praja Parishads to women in Andhra Pradesh.

THE ANDHRA PRADESH MANDAL PRAJA PARISHADS AND ZILLA PRAJA PARISHADS (RESERVATION OF OFFICES OF PRESIDENT OF MANDALA PRAJA PARISHADS AND CHAIRMAN OF ZILLA PRAJA PARISHADS) RULES, 1987

(G.O. Ms. No. 64, Panchayati Raj and Rural Development (Elections III), 3rd February, 1987)

In exercise of the powers conferred by sub-section (1) of Section 92 read with Sections 5, 44, and 91-A of the Andhra Pradesh Mandala Praja parishads, Zilla Praja Parishads and Zilla Abhivrudhi Sameeksha Mandala Act, 1986 (Act No. 31 of 1986), the Governor of Andhra Pradesh hereby makes the following rules relating to reservation of office of President, mandala Praja Parishads, Chairman, Zilla Praja Parishads for the Members belonging to Scheduled Tribes, Scheduled Castes, Women and Backward Classes.

RULES

1. **Short Title** — These rules may be called the Andhra Pradesh Mandala Praja Parishads and Zilla Praja Parishads (Reservation of offices of President of Mandala Praja Parishads and Chairman of Zilla Praja Parishads) Rules, 1987.

2. **Definitions** — In these rules, unless the context otherwise requires, —
   (i) 'Act' means of the Andhra Pradesh Mandal Praja Parishads, Zilla Praja Parishads and Zilla Abhivrudhi Sameeksha Mandals Act, 1986.
   (ii) words and expressions used but not defined in these rules shall have the meaning assigned to them in the Act.

3. **Reservation of offices of the President, Mandala Praja Parishads for the members belonging to Scheduled Tribes,**

Scheduled Castes, Women and Backward Classes— (1) The District Collector shall, subject to the provisions of these rules determine and notify "in the District Gazette" on tne same day on which the election notification is given, the number and the names of the Mandala Praja Parishads in the District, which shall be reserved for members belonging to Scheduled Tribes, Scheduled Castes, Women and Backward Classes for election of the offices of the President, Mandala Praja Parishads under Section 5 of the Act.

(2) While determining the number of offices of President, Mandala Praja Parishads to be reserved for the members belonging to Scheduled Tribes, Scheduled Castes, Women and Backward Classes any fraction less than one-half shall be ignored and any fraction equal to or more than one-half shall be counted as one.

(3) While determining the Mandala Praja Parishad in respect of which the office of the President is reserved for Scheduled Tribes, Schedule Castes.

4 (3) While determining the Zilla Praja Parishad in respect of which the office of Chairman is reserved for Scheduled Tribes, Scheduled Castes, Women and Backward Classes as the case may be the Zilla Praja Parishad so reserved as far as practicable be the District where the proportion of the population of the Scheduled Tribes, Scheduled Castes; Women or Backward Classes as the case may be to the total population of the District i.e., the largest in the descending order:

Provided that the reservation of the offices of the Chairman, Zilla Praja Parishads to all the categories put together in the state shall be in the ratio of 2:2:1 in respect of three regions of the state namely. Coastal Andhra, Telangana and Rayalaseema, respectively.

Appendix VIII

Extracts from The Andhra Pradesh Gram Panchayats act, 1964 as amended till date relating to representation of women in Gram Panchayats.

Section 9. Reservation of seats for women and members of Scheduled Castes and Scheduled Tribes:— (1) In every gram panchayat, out of the total strength thereof determined under Section 7, the Commissioner shall, subject to such rules as may be prescribed, by notification, reserve —

3 (a) two seats, if the total strength aforesaid is nine or less, three seats if the total strength aforesaid exceeds nine but does not exceed fifteen, and four seats if the total strength aforesaid exceeds fifteen for women.

Appendix IX

SCHEDULE

FOR FIELD WORK RELATING TO THE STUDY.

1. SOCIO—ECONOMIC BACKGROUND:

Name:
Age: Religion: Caste:

Educational Qualification; Profession Married/Unmarried/widowed.

No. of children if married.:

Husband's Profession :

Joint family/single family

Annual family income or property particulars:

Individual income or property of the member if any:

Household Duties:
Habits: (A) Listening to Radio (B) Reading News Papers
(C) Knitting (D) Embriodery
(E) Conversation with friends and relations (F) Gardening
(G) Social Service (H) Others.

Are you a member of any association other than political associations?

2. HUSBAND'S/FATHER'S/GUARDIAN'S INTEREST IN POLITICS AND SOCIAL SERVICES:

Is your husband/father/guardian interested in Politics? Yes/No.

If yes, does he attend political party meetings? Yes/No.

If attends, what is the intensity of attendance?
Rarely attends/attends now and then/frequently attends

Is he a member of any political party? Yes/No.

If yes, what is the position that he holds?

Is your husband/father/guardian a member of any cultural association/associations? Yes/No.

3. HUSBAND'S/FATHER'S/GUARDIAN'S ENCOURAGEMENT TO THE MEMBER:

How does your husband/father/guardian encourage you to participate in politics?

Does not like/neutral/encourages well

If there is encouragement, what is the nature of encouragement?

Permits to participate/accompanies

Other particulars if any:

4. IMPACT OF FAMILY, RELATIVES AND FRIENDS:

Do any of your family members, relations and friends participate in politics or in Social service or in both? Yes/No.

5. FACTORS THAT CONTRIBUTED TO ENTRANCE IN POLITICS:

When did you enter politics?

In which political institution have you first taken part?

Through whom did you enter politics?

How did you enter?

What factors contributed to your entering politics?

(A) Personal interest (B) Husband's/father's/guardian's encouragement

(C) Encouragement of friends (D) Other factors.

6. AWARENESS

How are the Gram Panchayats/Panchayat Samithis/Zilla Parishads Mandala Praja Parishads Constituted ?

What are the functions of the Gram Panchayats/Panchayat Samithis/Zilla Parishads Mandala Praja Parishads ?

Who was/is the President when you are a member of the Gram Panchayat/Panchayat Samithi/Mandala Praja Parishad/Zilla Parishad ?

How does the Executive Officer/Block Development Officer/ Collector help the functioning of the Gram Panchayat/Panchayat Samithi/Mandala Praja Parishad/Zilla Parishad ?

What are the functions of the Committee for Women Welfare ?

7. PARTICIPATION IN POLITICAL BODIES :

Did you contest in any elections ? Yes/No

If yes, for which position did you contest ?

Did you win ?

How do you attend the meetings of the political institution/ institutions in which you are a member ?

Rarely/now and then/frequently.

How do you participate in discussions ?

Does not participate/rarely participates/participates now and then/ frequently participates.

Did you initiate resolutions in the meetings ? Yes/No

If yes particulars:

What are the subjects of your interest in discussions ?

8. DECISION MAKING :

Who hold the key role in discussions ?

How are the decisions taken ?

9. ROLE OF OFFICIALS :

What role do the executive officers have in the functioning of the Panchayati Raj institutions ?

(A) Cooperate very much (B) Do not cooperate
(C) Hold key role in decisions (D) Other particulars

10. OTHER ASPECTS :

Are women members satisfactorily participating in the Panchayati Raj institutions? Yes/No

What should be done, in your opinion, to activise women's participation?

Do your participation in the household duties and participation in politics come into conflict with each other ?

Is it possible to all housewives to participate in politics ?

BIBLIOGRAPHY

BOOKS

Anuja Agarwal and D. R. Arora, *Women in Rural Society*, Vohra Publishers and Distributors, Allahabad, 1989.

Bhargava, B. S., *Emerging Leadership in Panchayati Raj System: A Study in a District of Rajasthan*, Institute of Social and Economic Change, Bangalore, 1977.

Darshankar, Arjun Y., *Leadership in Panchayati Raj: A Study of Beed District*, Panchasheel Prakashan, Jaipur, 1979.

ESCAP/FAO, *Learning from Rural Women*, Village Level Success Cases of Rural Women's Group Income Raising Activities, Inter-country Project for the Promotion of Training of Rural Women in Income Raising Group Activities, Bangkok, 1979.

Gaikwad, V. R., *Panchayati Raj and Bureaucracy: A Study of the Relationship Pattern*, National Institute of Community Development, Hyderabad, 1969.

Gautam Vohra, *Women in Bihar: A Study of Their Role in Tassar Silk Production*, Vikas Publishing House, New Delhi, 1988.

George, Jacob, (ed) *Readings on Panchayati Raj*, National Institute of Community Development, Hyderabad, 1967.

Government of Andhra Pradesh, Working Paper on Panchayati Raj Institutions, 1981.

Government of India, Committee on Plant Projects, Report of the Team for the Study of Community Projects and National Extension Service, 1957.

Government of India, Department of Rural Development, Ministry of Agriculture, Annual Report, 1986-87.

Government of India, Department of Rural Development, Ministry of Agriculture, Annual Report, 1987-88.

Government of India, Department of Rural Development, Ministry of Agriculture, Integrated Rural Development

Programme and Allied Programmes of Training of Rural Youth for Self-Employment (TRYSEM) and Development of Women and Children in Rural Areas (DWCRA): A Manual, 1987.

Government of India, Directorate of Extension, Ministry of Irrigation, Evaluation of the Farm Women Training Programme, Gwalior District, New Delhi. (unpublished)

Government of India, Integrated Rural Development Programme and Programmes of Training of Rural Youth for Self-Employment and Development of Women and Children in Rural Areas, New Delhi, 1987.

Government of India, Ministry of Human Resource Development, Department of Women and Child Welfare, National Perspective Plan for Women 1988-2000 A.D., Report of the Core Group, Akashdeep Printers, New Delhi, 1988.

Government of India, Ministry of Rural Development, Ministry of Agriculture, Report of the Committee to Review the Administrative Arrangements for Rural Development and Poverty Alleviation Programmes (G. V. K. Rao Committee's Report), New Delhi, 1985.

Government of India, *Panchayati Raj at a Glance*, Status of Panchayati Raj Institutions in India, 1987-88, Krishi Bhavan, New Delhi, 1989.

Government of India, Report of the Committee on Panchayati Raj, 1978.

Government of West Bengal, Department of Panchayats and Community Development, *Panchayats in West Bengal from 1978-79 to 1980-81, A Review*, 1982.

Government of West Bengal, *Dynamics of the Rural Situation in West Bengal Panchayati Raj*, 1978.

Gupta, J. L. (ed) *Challenges to the Fair Sex: Indian Women: Problems, Plights and Progresses*, Gian Publishing House, Delhi, 1988.

Halef Afshar, *Women, State and Ideology*, Macmillan, London, 1987.

Haragopal, G., *Administrative Leadership and Rural Development in India*, Light and Life Publishers, New Delhi, 1980.

Hargian Singh, *Rural Political System in India*, Indira Publishers, Gurgaon, 1985.

Hazel D'Lima, *Women in Local Government: A Study of*

Maharashtra, Concept Publishing Company, New Delhi, 1983.

Indira Awasty, *Rural Women in India*, Gupta Printing Press, New Delhi, 1982.

International Labour Office, *Women in Rural Development: Critical Issues*, Geneva, 1980.

Jain, S.P., *Panchayati Raj in Assam*, National Institute of Community Development, Hyderabad, 1976.

Jain, S.P. and Krishnamurthy Reddy V., *Role of Women in Rural Development: A Study of Mahila Mandals*, National Institute of Rural Development, Hyderabad, 1979.

Janet, A Flammang (ed) *Political Women: Current Roles in State and Local Governments*, Sage Publications, New Delhi, 1984.

Kalpana Raghuvanshi, *Rural Women in Rajasthan*, Kanchenjunga Publications, Jaipur, 1983.

Kaur, Satnam, *Women in Rural Development*, Mittal Publications, New Delhi, 1987.

Krishna Iyer, *Women Unbound: A Plea for Gender Justice*, Society for Community Organisation Trust, Madurai, 1984.

Lakshminarayana, H. D., *Rural Legislators in an Indian State*, Inter-India Publications, New Delhi, 1985.

Mahila Chetna Manch, *Women and Children in Madhya Pradesh: A Profile*, Bhopal, 1985.

Maitrayee Mukhopadhyay, *Silver Shackles: Women and Development in India*, Parchment (Oxford) Ltd., Oxford, 1984.

Majumdar, Vina, (ed) *Role of Rural Women in Development*, Report of an International Seminar, 1978.

Majumdar, Vina (ed), *Symbols of Power*, Allied Publishers Pvt. Ltd., New Delhi, 1979.

Mariana Githens and Prestage Jewel L. (ed), *A Portrait of Marginality: The Political Behaviour of American Women*, Longman, New York, 1977.

Martha F. Loufti, *Rural Women: Unequal Partners in Development*, International Labour Office, Geneva, 1982.

Mathew, George (ed), *Panchayati Raj in Karnataka Today*, Institute of Social Sciences and Concepting Publishing Company, New Delhi, 1986.

Mathew, P.M. and Nair M.S., *Women's Organisations and Women's Interests*, Ashish Publishing House, New Delhi, 1986.

Mathur, Kuldeep, *Bureaucratic Response to Development*, National Publishing House, New Delhi, 1972.

Mats, Kihlberg, *The Panchayati Raj of India*, Young Asia Publications, New Delhi, 1970.

Maurya, S.D. (ed), *Women in India*, Chugh Publications, Allahabad, 1988.

Mumtaz Ali Khan and Noor Ayesha, *Status of Rural Women in India: A Study of Karnataka*, Uppal Publishing House, New Delhi, 1987.

National Institute of Public Cooperation and Child Development, *Handbook of Policy and Related Documents on Women in India*, New Delhi, 1988.

Panikkar, K.K., *Community Development in Kerala*, S. Chand & Co. Pvt. Ltd., New Delhi, 1974.

Planning Commission, Programme Evaluation Organisation, *Some Successful Panchayats: Case Studies*, 1960.

Raghava Rao, *Panchayats and Rural Development*, Ashish Publishing House, New Delhi, 1980.

Rajput, R.S. (ed), *Panchayati Raj in India: Democracy at Grassroots*, Deep and Deep Publications, New Delhi, 1984.

Rajput, R.S. and D.R. Meghe (ed), *Panchayati Raj in India: Democracy at Grassroots*, Deep and Deep Publications, New Delhi, 1984.

Rama, K.G. *Women Welfare in Tamil Nadu*, Sangam Publishers, Madras (for Madras Institute of Development Studies), 1974.

Ranjana Kumari, *Women Headed Households in Rural India*, Radiant Publishers, New Delhi, 1989.

Rao, U.N.J. *Women in a Developing Society*, Asish Publishing House, New Delhi, 1985.

Reddy, Ram, G. (ed) *Patterns of Panchayati Raj in India*, The Macmillan Company of India Ltd., New Delhi, 1977.

Rehana Ghadially, *Women in Indian Society*, Sage Publications, New Delhi, 1988.

Rekhadevi Raju, *Status of Women*, Dastane Ramachandra Rao & Co., Poona, 1988.

Rekha Mehra and Saradamoni K, *Women and Rural Transformation*, Concept, New Delhi, 1982.

Reston, James, *American Women in Public Life Today*, Peggy Lamson, Haughton, Boston, 1968.

Shanti Kothari and Ramashray Roy, *Relation Between Politicians and Administrators at the District Level*, Indian Institute of Public Administration, New Delhi, 1981.

Sharada Jain, Mamta Jaitly, Kavita Srivastava, Nirmala Nair and Kanchan Mathur, *Exploiting Possibilities: A Review of Women's Development Programme*, Rajasthan, Institute of Development Studies, Jaipur, 1988.

Shivayya M., *Panchayati Raj : A Policy Perspective*, National Institute of Rural Development , Hyderabad, 1986.

Subramanian, R. (ed), *Rural Development: An Inside Look at Problems and Prospects*, Yatan Publications, New Delhi, 1988.

Sugata Das Gupta and L. S. N. Murthy, *Panchayati Raj Institutions in West Bengal*, National Institute of Public Cooperation and Child Development, New Delhi, 1983.

Sushama Sahay Prasad, *Tribal Women Labourers: Aspects of Economic and Physical Exploitation*, Gian Publishing House, Delhi, 1988.

Sushila Agarwal (ed), *Status of Women*, Printwell Publishers, Jaipur, 1988.

Tak, B.L., *Sociological Dimensions of Gram Raj*, Vimal Prakashan, Ghaziabad, 1973.

Talunkar, Atul Chandra, *Political Transition in Grassroots in Tribal India*, Omsons Publications, New Delhi, 1987.

United Nations Organisation, *Report of the Secretary General on the Participation of Women in Community Development*, New York, 1972.

Vasudeva Rao, D. (ed), *Rural Development: An Overview*, Sri Satguru Publications, Delhi, 1986.

Whyte Robert Orr and Pauline Whyte, *The Women of Rural Asia*, West View Press, Boulder, Colorado, USA, 1982.

White, Theodore H., *New Power, New Politics: The American Review*, Summer, 1984.

UNPUBLISHED WORKS

Amareswari K, Inaugural Address at the IV National Conference on Women's Studies on Rural Women: Poverty, Survival and Struggle for Change held at Waltair, Andhra Pradesh, 1988.

Annie Nirmal K., "Rural Women's Struggle for Existence: A Cast Study of the Indian Rural Women in Gulf Countries," A Paper presented at the IV National Conference on Women's Studies, Waltair, Andhra Pradesh, 1988.

Ila Pathak, Presidential Address at the IV National Conference on "Women's Studies on Rural Women: Poverty, Survivial and Struggle for Change," held at Waltair, Andhra Pradesh, 1988.

Maithreyi Krishna Raj and Divya Pandey, "Women Assist Change by not Assisting Themselves?" A Paper presented at the IV National Conference on Women's Studies, Waltair, Andhra Pradesh, 1988.

Manikyamba P., "Participation of Women in Panchayati Raj: A Case Study of one Zilla Parishad," Two Panchayat Samithis and Four Gram Panchayats in Andhra Pradesh, 1980.

Manikyamba P., "Women in Panchayati Raj: Premises and Performance," A Paper presented at a Seminar on District Administration organised in March 1988 by Shaheed Bhagat Singh College, New Delhi.

Naidu, N. Y. and S. P. Jain, "Panchayati Raj and Social Change: A Study in Assam," 1978.

Nalini Nayak, "Technology Change, the Labour Process and Employment in Relation to Women in the Fishing Sector," A Paper presented at the IV National Conference on Women's Studies, Waltair, Andhra Pradesh, 1988.

Nirmala Kumari S., "Increasing Work Burden of Rural Women in Changing Environment of Villages," A Paper presented at the IV National Conference on Women's Studies, Waltair, Andhra Pradesh, 1988.

Nita Shirali, Sumitra Das Gupta and Abhijit Das Gupta, "Women in the Silk Industries of Bengal," A Paper presented at the IV National Conference on Women's Studies, Waltair, Andhra Pradesh, 1988.

Rajaput Pam, "Women's Leadership at the Grass-roots Level in the Punjab," A Paper present at the IV National Conference on Women's Studies, Waltair, Andhra Pradesh, 1988.

Rekha Mehra, "The Neglect of Women in India's Rural Development Programmes — A Study of Failures in Planning," 1979.

Sahul Marnie S., "The Status of Women in Local Governments Around the World," A Paper presented to a Working Group of International Union of Local Authorities, Columbus, Ohio, USA, 1981.

Sriranjani Subba Rao K., "Role of Women in the Panchayati Raj Institutions," A Paper presented at the IV National Concerence on Women's Studies at Waltair, Andhra Pradesh, 1988.

ARTICLES

Amal Ray and Jayalakshmi Kumpatla, Zilla Parishad Presidents in Karnataka: Their Social Background and Implications for Development, *Economic and Political Weekly*, Oct. 17-24, 1984.

A Report of the Workshop on Integrated Rural Development Programme and Development of Women and Children in rural Areas, *Prajnan*, Vol. XII, No. 4, Oct-Dec. 1983.

Chandrasekhara Rao, R. V. R., Some Aspects of Reorganisation of District Administration in Andhra Pradesh, *Journal of the Society for the Study of State Governments*, Vol. II, Oct-Dec. 1969.

Dikshit A.P., and Aradhana Chek, Women and Rural Development in India, *Kurukshetra*, Vol. XXXIV, No. 3, Dec. 1985.

Gurmeet Dhillon, Rural Women in Decision Making Action, *Kurukshetra*, Vol. XXVIII, No. 9, Ist February, 1980.

Janaki Nair, Karnataka Zilla Parishad Presidents, *Economic and Political Weekly*, Vol. XXII, No. 4, January 24th, 1987.

Krishna Iyer, Women's Lot in Fact, *Voluntary Action*, Vol. 26, No. 102, July-August, 1983.

Narayana Rao K.V., Gram Panchayats in Andhra Pradesh, *Community Development and Panchayati Raj Digest*, Vol. V, No. 4, 1976.

Patil, V.T., and A.T. Kittur, An Analysis of Official-Non Official Relations in the Panchayats, *Kurukshetra*, April 1986.

Paul Radha, Women's Leadership in welfare Work, *Social Welfare*, Vol. XXVII, No. 3, June 1980.

Reddy, Ram G., Social Composition of Panchayati Raj: Background of Political Executives in Andhra Pradesh, *Economic and Political Weekly*, Vol. II, 1967.

Sarala Gopalam, Why are Women lagging behind? *Kurukshetra*, December, 1987.

Saxena, K.B., Panchayats and Women, *Kurukshetra*, Vol. XXXVII, February, 1989.

Theodore H. White, *New Power, New Politics, The American Review*, Summer, 1984.

Index